# GAIN Positive and Mindful Self-Leadership

Joan Marques

# GAIN Positive and Mindful Self-Leadership

Toward Purpose Driven Insights

Joan Marques
School of Business
Woodbury University
Burbank, CA, USA

ISBN 978-3-031-63824-4     ISBN 978-3-031-63825-1  (eBook)
https://doi.org/10.1007/978-3-031-63825-1

© The Editor(s) (if applicable) and The Author(s), under exclusive license to Springer Nature Switzerland AG 2024

This work is subject to copyright. All rights are solely and exclusively licensed by the Publisher, whether the whole or part of the material is concerned, specifically the rights of translation, reprinting, reuse of illustrations, recitation, broadcasting, reproduction on microfilms or in any other physical way, and transmission or information storage and retrieval, electronic adaptation, computer software, or by similar or dissimilar methodology now known or hereafter developed.

The use of general descriptive names, registered names, trademarks, service marks, etc. in this publication does not imply, even in the absence of a specific statement, that such names are exempt from the relevant protective laws and regulations and therefore free for general use.

The publisher, the authors and the editors are safe to assume that the advice and information in this book are believed to be true and accurate at the date of publication. Neither the publisher nor the authors or the editors give a warranty, expressed or implied, with respect to the material contained herein or for any errors or omissions that may have been made. The publisher remains neutral with regard to jurisdictional claims in published maps and institutional affiliations.

This Springer imprint is published by the registered company Springer Nature Switzerland AG
The registered company address is: Gewerbestrasse 11, 6330 Cham, Switzerland

If disposing of this product, please recycle the paper.

The supreme beauty of life
is also its greatest difficulty:
Understanding that nothing here is really ours
and that every moment can be our last.
Similarly, we should embrace
that nothing here is wasted
and that every experience
fits into our life's cast.
We can use this reality
as an insight to rejoice
or one to grief.
We create our own reality
so, the choice is ours
and that's a relief.

~ Joan Marques

# Foreword

GAIN is a perspective on life that is truly worth embracing. As we mature, it becomes clear to us that no experience was a wasted one, and that everything we went through contributed to the person we ultimately became.

On a daily basis we generate, appreciate, internalize, and rise to newness, even though we don't always pay this process the attention it deserves. Joan Marques' inclusion of Vipassana meditation as a non-sectarian way to retrain our mind toward identifying and subsequently releasing our suffering is therefore critical in this book.

Using life snapshots of well-known people in our society, and some lesser known ones who made admirable strides, enhances the pleasure of understanding the construct Dr. Marques presents in this work.

As a strong believer in the spiritual foundations of our common existence on this planet, I find great value in the concept of interbeing that is explained in this book. There is so much we should be grateful for regarding our interconnectedness, and that, too, is something we must contemplate on more often, in a similar way as we should do regarding our breathing and its representation of the arising and passing of everything. Most people may feel somewhat anxious at first to think of their daily existence in that light, as no one likes the concept of passing unless it pertains to something we want to release. Yet, understanding both, interbeing and the arising and passing of everything will keep us grounded, and help us release some of the stress we acquire when we want to hold on to a status quo that is no longer sensible.

As a long-time crisis management authority, I have learned that, like everything else in life, crises are also interrelated, oftentimes to aspects and actions we don't consider, or simply underestimate. Awareness, communication, and reflection are key in that regard, as well as in every other aspect of our lives.

In recent months, I have been writing short articles on LinkedIn discussing the concerns of coping with a troubled and messy world. Given the many social commotions we learn about on an almost daily basis, I can only hope that our upcoming generations will be spared from the tell-tale signs of increased mental instability, which leads not only to lasting ailments but also to increasing suicidal tendencies.

With Artificial Intelligence being one of the main areas of interest in this era, we are facing claims of some groups that AI will attain consciousness. Considering the fact that human beings need a lifetime of continuous practice to elevate our awareness and maintain our mental and emotional health, I am highly concerned about the direction of attributing Human Intelligence to the limited Cognitive Intelligence of AI.

Human-made devices could and will not be able to attain what was granted to us, and we should cherish that insight, rather than allowing ourselves to be led astray in our excitement about the new tendency of the day.

Rather than becoming our own enemy, we should return to the appreciation of life as it has been granted to us, and work on elevating our own awareness toward respect for all those sharing this planet with us.

With all that is going on in our world today, we collectively need to regain our sense of inner connection, in order to cherish our interconnection. I am therefore warmly recommending you to read this book, and use GAIN in your end-of-day contemplations, so that you can continue to maintain awareness of the *generating* process of experiences, the *appreciation* of those experiences, even if they may not always seem rosy at first, and the *internalization* of these experiences toward attaining a better understanding on how they can contribute to the *newness* that we need to make this world the peaceful, interconnected, collectively embracing home it is to us all.

Founder and President of Mitroff Crisis Management, Senior Research Affiliate, Center for Catastrophic Risk Management, UC Berkeley, Professor Emeritus, Marshall School of Business & Annenberg School of Communication, University of Southern California
Los Angeles, CA, USA

Ian I. Mitroff

# Contents

1 Life Happens to All of Us .................................................. 1

2 Breathing = Life (and So Much More) ........................... 17

3 Life Is All GAIN ................................................................ 29

4 Generating: The Experiences Life Presents Us .............. 41

5 Appreciating: Valuing the Experiences ........................... 53

6 Internalizing: Bringing It All into Scope ....................... 67

7 Newness: Rebirth Through Enrichment ........................ 83

8 Practices and Exercises Supporting GAIN .................... 99

9 Leading with a GAIN Focus ............................................ 113

10 A Mindful Journey ........................................................... 131

Index ........................................................................................ 145

# 1

# Life Happens to All of Us

**Contents**
Being Grateful for Our Gifts .................................................................................... 3
Three Self-Erected Roadblocks ................................................................................ 6
Evaluating Setbacks ................................................................................................ 12
Chapter Highlights ................................................................................................. 16

**Abstract** This chapter lays the groundwork of the book, which relates to the understanding that life is a matter of perceived ups and downs, all serving a purpose toward future wholesomeness that none of us can see or comprehend on the short run. It invites you to reflect on your life and question what progresses and defeats/losses you encountered. It also invites you to reframe your negative experiences by thinking of at least three ways in which the "downsides" still brought something good at this stage of your life.

**We're All Winners: A Story**
Under a large plumbago bush lived a large family of ground squirrels. They had a lot of fun together, especially with the young ones growing up so rapidly and finding their ways in the gardens where they looked for seeds and fruits.

Three of the young squirrels, Shirley, Furley and Pearly, always hung out together. Shirley and Furley seemed to become really good at finding seeds, and they got a lot of compliments from the older squirrels for their feisty and go-getting attitude. Pearly, who was a little smaller than her sisters, was not as fast or aggressive and often only found some leftovers.

One day, Shirley and Furley were eagerly filling their cheeks with seeds to take home, while Pearly patiently waiting to get her share. Suddenly she saw a hawk flying in, ready to snatch up Furley from behind. Pearly let out a high pitched squeak, the way only ground squirrels can do, and it was loud enough to distract the hawk and alert Shirley and Furley about the impending danger. The hawk quickly flew up and away and the three young squirrels hurried back to the safety of the plumbago bush.

That day, everyone praised Pearly for her brave interference, and she got an extra portion of seeds as reward. Shirley and Furley thanked her abundantly, and from that day on, all the squirrels had deep respect for Pearly's attentiveness and bravery.

> The squirrels realized that everyone has different talents, and that we should never take anyone for granted. Success cannot be measured in just one way. Pearly thought them that.

---

> Life isn't about finding yourself. Life is about creating yourself.[1]
> ~*George Bernard Shaw*

### A Beautiful Day

The sun smiles at the dancing butterflies
As clouds play tag in the heavenly skies

A hummingbird dwells on a honey source
A canoe explores the river course

An older couple holds hands on the bench
A little boy launches his boat in the trench

An open window releases the guitar song
A mother goes shopping – her tot tags along

A businessman's bribing his way to the top
The light just turned red – the car wheels now stop

---

[1] https://www.brainyquote.com/quotes/george_bernard_shaw_109542

The homeless holds up his rough hand for a dime
A nerd formulates a definition of 'crime'

A baby is born and a new mom is made
A gardener takes a quick break in the shade

A cat takes a bath and then yawns long and broad
An auditor detects a huge company fraud

A woman in high heels forgets who she was
A dog licks itself the way every dog does

The mountains are clear but the air smells like rain
The crowd in the station awaits the next train

The peace demonstration is peaceful and quiet
The reporter's bummed because there's no riot

A lazy man wants to invent something great
He hopes that his bright idea won't come too late

The drive-through is busy – the crowd wants to eat
It's rush hour – the traffic is jammed in the street

Soon it will be night and the folks will be home
Except for those watching the game in the dome

Then... it's time for bed – what a great place to stay
It's the end of an ordinary yet beautiful day

*–Joan Marques*

## Being Grateful for Our Gifts

What do Einstein, Edison, and Steve Jobs have in common? Much more than the major credits of how they changed the world through their inventions. Their early life was in no way a prediction of the success they would have later. They were not apparently "gifted" from the get-go. Albert Einstein was three before he could speak decently, he was clumsy and therefore not very successful in his first years in grammar school. As he progressed through school, indications of his intelligence started surfacing. Yet, his early years as a young man were turbulent, marked by school drop-outs, job losses, and failure to start a teaching career due to a poor recommendation.[2] Fortunately, Einstein was always great in mathematics, and that turned out to be an early prediction of his later success in the world-changing theory of relativity and other impressive accomplishments. Till this day, Einstein is known as the most influential physicist of the twentieth century.

Thomas Edison only attended school for a few months, as his mother, who was a teacher, decided to homeschool him. Whether he was slow or simply troubled by illness is not entirely clear, but there is reason to believe that his early years were not very revealing of the genius he was later declared to be. Edison developed hearing problems from an early age on, most likely due to a family tendency to get middle ear infections. Some observants said that Edison's deafness strongly influenced his behavior and career, providing the motivation for many of his inventions.[3] There is a famous story of his many failed attempts before developing the lightbulb, and his mindful perspective on those attempts. He preferred not to see them as failures, but as evidence of the many ways things did not work out. In the end, he turned out to be a man with more than 1000 patents, and a number of impressive inventions to his name, among which the electric light bulb, phonograph, and batteries.

Steve Jobs also had a rocky intellectual start. Raised by adoptive parents in Cupertino, California, he had his share of problems in school, albeit not because of seeming dull-mindedness, but rather because of being bored, misbehaving, and averse to authority. Jobs dropped out of Reed College in Oregon, worked for the Atari Corporation as a video game designer in 1974, and then decided to make a pilgrimage to India to experience Buddhism.[4] Yet, throughout his adventures and school drop-outs, Jobs managed to gather the right knowledge and establish the right connections to experiment – and succeed – with computers. His career is one of the better known, and his legendary return to Apple after being ousted, sealed his success with a string of highly popular devices among which the iMac, the iPod, the iPad, and of course, the iPhone.

---

[2] Kaku, M. (Jan. 9, 2024). Albert Einstein – German-American Physicist. *Britannica*. Retrieved from https://www.britannica.com/biography/Albert-Einstein/General-relativity-and-teaching-career
[3] Josephson, M. & Conot, R. (Dec. 25, 2023). Thomas Edison – American Inventor. *Britannica*. Retrieved from https://www.britannica.com/biography/Thomas-Edison
[4] Levy, S. (Jan. 9, 2024). Steve Jobs – American Businessman. *Britannica*. Retrieved from https://www.britannica.com/biography/Steve-Jobs

## 1  Life Happens to All of Us      5

What I most appreciate about these three men is their encouraging outlook on life, which can be detected in some of their publicly available quotes. Among the many things Einstein said, the following quote captures his insight in what really matters in life very well:

*Everybody is a genius. But if you judge a fish by its ability to climb a tree, it will live its whole life believing that it is stupid.*[5]

Reflecting on his own numerous failures before succeeding, Edison said,

*Many of life's failures are people who did not realize how close they were to success when they gave up.*[6]

Steve Jobs, oftentimes described as a loner, sometimes as a bully or a hard-nosed person, once uttered the following reflective statement:

*Don't let the noise of others' opinions drown out your own inner voice.*[7]

Like all of us, Einstein, Edison and Jobs definitely had their moments of self-doubt, their periods of depression, and their fear tat they might not have been on the right track, but I believe they worked on these cloudy influences that can get a firm hold on us, and they shook them off, like the donkey who had fallen in an old dry pit, and brayed loudly until his owner, an old farmer, heard him. The farmer, who lived alone with no direct neighbors close by, first looked for ways to release the donkey, and could not find anything that would work. In despair, he ultimately decided to throw dirt in the pit. As the dirt started hitting the donkey's back, he first got upset, suspecting that his owner wanted to bury him alive. However, after some time he abandoned the gloomy thoughts, started shaking off the dirt and stepping on it. With every shake and step he got a bit higher, until he could finally step out of the pit.

Indeed, there is no victory in hanging your head when a load of life's lemons hits you. Tapping into your inner sweets to convert the lemons into lemonade is a skill that you can learn. And I am well aware that it's not always easy to do, because some surprises are so unforeseen and devastating that you may feel as if the wind was sucked out of your sails. Time is an important friend in this regard, however: as the days go by, you can learn how to shift your lenses

---

[5] https://www.azquotes.com/quote/369274
[6] https://www.brainyquote.com/quotes/thomas_a_edison_109004
[7] https://www.azquotes.com/quote/458474

and start looking at the new situation from a variety of angles until you discover a way to cope with it, and hopefully even transform it into a blessing.

*Daniel was an energetic man in his late thirties, with a large family, and a great set of brains. He had been working as a professor of Information Technology at a small institution in California, and was good at what he was doing. Gradually, however, he realized that he had another passion: Accounting. He also saw that there was a need for accountants in the education field. So, Daniel picked up studying accounting, and in two years acquired the credentials to serve as both an accounting and an IT professor. Unfortunately, he learned that his school, while optimally using all his skills, was not willing to pay for his newly acquired qualifications. Daniel decided that it was time to start exploring the horizon. He soon received a job offer at the east coast, which meant uprooting his family. The choice was not easy, but it was not insurmountable either. Daniel said goodbye to his friends, family, and colleagues, took his family with him, and ceased the opportunity. He had made the decision for multiple reasons, aside from the undervaluing approach from his previous employer. With life far less expensive in his new city, Daniel could afford a home that was three times the size of the one he and his family had been occupying in California. He kept in touch with some of his old friends, but also made new ones in his new environment, and realizes now that he made the right move.*

## Three Self-Erected Roadblocks

Being the smart beings we are, we have an equal ability to break through boundaries and to create them. Oftentimes we are more aware of boundaries that we need to break than we are about the ones we unwillingly erected. Still, there are numerous ways in which we create and uphold mental roadblocks that inhibit our progress. Let's look at three common mental roadblocks we erect as we go through our daily routines.

1. *Sleepwalking*

    When you go through your days without ever taking a moment to reflect on your circumstances, your behavior, the things you discussed, the decisions you made, their outcomes, and whether your life as it currently runs is really how you would like it, you are sleepwalking. It's not a shameful thing, because we are all guilty of doing it at times, especially when there is so much going on that we have difficulty keeping up with the speed of things that come and go. What would be shameful is to keep on sleepwalking once you become aware that you are doing it.

The idea is not for you to reflect all the time on everything, but if you can at least take a few minutes, possibly at the end of your day, to reflect on the things that went on and how you felt about them, you might surprise yourself in future actions and behaviors. Reflection helps you catch yourself doing good and bad things, and provides you the mental insight to adjust your acts where needed.

Reflecting is especially valuable when you find yourself at a crossroads: when you become aware of that gnawing sense of discomfort about your life and take the time to analyze what you should change about it. Let me be frank: sometimes you may not like your findings, as the logical solution may be one that is hard to realize. If, for instance, you find out that your marriage or relationship has become a dull routine, you will most likely consider options to do something about it, and the alternatives can vary from having a good talk with your spouse or partner and deciding on some constructive changes, to starting to see a therapist, or splitting up in cases where things seem hopeless. If the problem is your job, you may also have to consider options, varying from requesting transfer to a different department, getting the training needed to become eligible for a promotion, or finding other employment.

A number of years ago Forbes published an article on career sleepwalkers: people that aimlessly wander from job to job and are in search for their passion, but don't know exactly what they're looking for. The author of the article confirmed that the number of career sleepwalkers is growing, with 37% of employees claiming they have no sense of a career path, and 23% saying they feel like they are on a treadmill going nowhere. As a result, 80% of employees under 24 would consider switching careers. The article calls for managers to take positive advantage of this trend by

A) Helping these employees find their purpose. Introducing the practice of reflecting to these employees would be an excellent first step, because that might help them identify their strengths;
B) Encouraging risk-taking, even if it doesn't mean a promotion. Every change in the workplace means gaining new experience and learning new things. In those shifts, employees may discover their area of passion. They may get inspired and become really good at a specific task they may have never thought of;
C) Creating space for continuous learning, because that provides the impetus for exploring new avenues. Managers are encouraged to allow their employees to partake in training sessions and seminars on topics of their interest, as these may also lead to increased passion, and

D) Serving as career coaches: while most managers may not see themselves as career coaches, they could encourage their employees to visit HR for input on training opportunities in multiple areas.[8]

At any rate, the awareness that you have been sleepwalking leads to the realization that you need to undertake some actions, and that's where you can run into the next roadblock: comfort zone clinging.

2. *Comfort Zone Clinging*

Sometimes you know exactly what you need to do to change an undesirable situation, but the action that is called for seems too cumbersome. We are creatures of habit and don't like change, especially not when it comes to major parts of our lives such as home, work, or any other routine we have become accustomed to. People can get used to almost anything, even circumstances that are far from pleasant. Dr. Abigail Brenner, a psychiatrist, describes a comfort zone as a psychological/emotional/behavior construct that defines the routine of our daily life that implies familiarity, safety, and security.[9] We have constructed our comfort zone, and there are many reasons why we cling to it. Most of the time it is fear about the unknown that keeps us where we are. You may have heard someone say, "you know what you got, but you don't know what you'll be getting when you change things." The consideration here is, that the current situation, regardless how undesirable, requires a set of behaviors that you have now mastered, while a new situation will require deconstructing your current behaviors and reconstructing new ones, and who knows how difficult that learning process might be!

Sometimes the fear to leave the current comfort zone may be one instilled by others. This doesn't have to be done with malicious intent. A loving parent, for instance, may want to hold on to keep their young adult son or daughter around, even though they really yearn for further education in a more suitable place. In some cases, however, there may be self-centered or even malicious intent, such as a controlling partner who doesn't want to let go of the one they are taking advantage of.

There is no key advice to be given here, because breaking away from what you are used to is just not easy. The only thing that may help is cau-

---

[8] Bersin, J. (Aug. 152018). Career Sleepwalkers: Who They Are and How to Wake Them Up. *Forbes: Leadership*. Retrieved from https://www.forbes.com/sites/joshbersin/2018/08/15/career-sleepwalkers-who-they-are-and-how-to-wake-them-up/?sh=7907d3f95069

[9] Brenner, A. (Dec. 222015). 5 Benefits of Stepping Outside Your Comfort Zone. *Psychology Today*. Retrieved from https://www.psychologytoday.com/us/blog/in-flux/201512/5-benefits-stepping-outside-your-comfort-zone

tion. You can try to shine some light on the darkness you are supposed to leap into by exploring. If, for instance, you plan to move to another city, state or country, try to visit the place a few times to explore the environment and get acquainted with some people and places. If you aim to embark upon a new job, try reading about this new work environment and what the general comments are. Be mindful of what's written, but don't get overly stressed by some less favorable comments. Remember, it's always the disgruntled few that take to the net with their negativity. A friend of mine who ran a popular restaurant told me that customers are the most interesting people: they can visit you 100 times with good results, but the one time something is off, they take to the Net to share their dissatisfaction. As a long time professor I have discovered similar patterns among students: the ones with a satisfactory experience will remain silent in their course evaluations, but the ones who received a lower grade than they desired, will spout their disgruntlement in every possible detail at the most visible forum they can find.

Like with everything in life, there are pros and cons to comfort zones. I came across some great arguments for both sides on a University website. The article underscores my above arguments about the need to understand that we have a comfort zone, and that we sometimes must step out of it to expand our horizons. Undoubtedly there are advantages of staying in your comfort zone, otherwise you would not create it. Some of these advantages are:

- Familiarity: Your comfort zone is a familiar place, and it consists of things you have done many times before, so you can draw on your experience in the implementation of your actions.
- Confidence: Because you have the familiarity of people, places and actions in your comfort zone, you have less stress and feel more confident.
- Low risk: Since you pretty much know your way around in your comfort zone, it's not a risky environment.
- Comforting: Your comfort zone is a nice place to return to when you have made some excursions into new territories, and it allows you to recuperate from any stress you may have endured while elsewhere.
- Energy saving: Because the things you do in your comfort zone are mostly familiar, they demand less of your energy, so you have more mental space to explore other things.[10]

And then there are the cons of staying in your comfort zone, some of which are:

- Lethargic: If you don't undertake any steps outside your comfort zone, you shortchange your own development and opportunities in life.
- No advancement: Wallowing in the same old circle and status quo doesn't teach you anything new, and doesn't expose you to new opportunities for development. With that, you curtail your options and possible advancement.

---

[10] *The Pros and Cons of Comfort Zones* (Oct. 222022). *Walden University.* Retrieved from https://www.waldenu.edu/programs/psychology/resource/the-pros-and-cons-of-comfort-zones

- Narrow views: By not learning anything new, you withhold yourself from new chances and exciting directions that might open new pathways of development for you.
- Limiting capacities: Staying in your comfort zone also means that you don't develop any new skills toward exciting new opportunities.
- Keeping your comfort zone small: If you don't step out of it, you will keep your comfort zone limited. When you dare to step out of it, you you're your areas of familiarity, and with that, you also expand your comfort zone into new territories.[11]

### 3. *Implicit Biases*

We all acquire predispositions throughout our lives. Some ideas are instilled by the people who raised us, or by peers in school, by members of groups we belong to, or others. Implicit bias often leads to quick labeling of a large group of people based on one encounter or the behavior of one person. This is how people develop opinions about others that are completely unfounded, and can be harmful for both, the judger and the one judged.

People who are judged based on the behavior or traits of one poor experience with a member of the (e.g. ethnic, age, gender, religious, or cultural) group they belong to may experience unjustified rejection when applying for a job or being ostracized in a workplace and therefore unable to establish deeper levels of collegiality.

When you judge others on basis of implicit biases, you deprive yourself from some great opportunities to expand your horizons and work with a more diverse group of people. You thereby also limit your prospects to become privy of other insights that could be valuable in future situations.

Because implicit biases are sometimes deeply rooted, it may take some conscientious reflection to confront your thought patterns and their foundations. The problem is that you may sometimes find that people who you deeply love, honor, and respect have contributed to your bias, and that can be a tough perspective to internalize. Just remember that all humans are flawed, and that your mentor, friend, or parent who planted the seed of this bias in your mind may be struggling with blind spots that they will have to address for themselves. You don't have to confront people to forgive them for their negative influence. Once you have acquired insight and clarity, there is simply too much to celebrate, as you have liberated yourself from a strangling mindset that would only limit your opportunities in life. And that is reason for being happy enough (Fig. 1.1).

---

[11] Ibid.

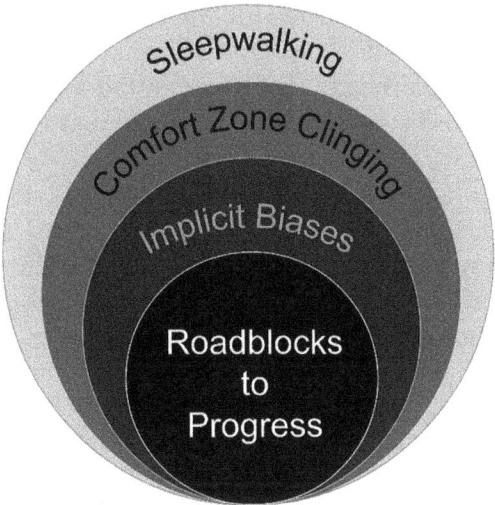

**Fig. 1.1** Roadblocks to progress

In an interesting article on implicit biases and whether we can overcome them, Dr. McCauley admits that this could be a daunting task, because our behaviors are subconsciously influenced by our implicit cognition. This means that, even if we are educated toward different perceptions, our implicit biases can sometimes overrule our educated insights. Changing implicit biases may, in cases of strong embedding, require deep scrutiny and consequential reconstruction of an entire community's general stance.[12]

Interestingly, Dr. Lawrence White discusses an impressive Harvard University cognitive bias test ("The Implicit Association Test", IAT) that was conducted in 2016 over three consecutive days amongst 5295 non-Black undergraduates at 18 university campuses. In the test, which is still freely available online, participants were challenged to at time link positive qualities to white people and negative qualities to black people, and at other times link negative qualities to white people and positive ones to black people. The study showed that over the course of the three test-days, there was a slight change in bias levels, but that the overarching biases of the participants did not significantly change over time.

However, two social psychologists from the University of North Carolina questioned the above presented study findings and decided to take a look at the environmental factors of the 18 universities involved. Their analysis

---

[12] McCauley, R. N. (Nov. 272016). Can People Overcome Their Implicit Biases? *Psychology Today*. Retrieved from https://www.psychologytoday.com/us/blog/why-religion-is-natural-and-science-is-not/201611/can-people-overcome-their-implicit-biases

demonstrated a strong influence of these environmental factors. They found that there was a higher level of racist biases amongst students from campuses with confederate statues (representing white supremacy), and a lower level of such biases amongst students from campuses with greater diversity.

The two social psychologists concluded that implicit bias is more a result of surrounding environments and influences than of individual belief. In other words: environments that encourage discriminatory mindsets will yield higher levels of biases (in this case racial bias) amongst their community members than environments with greater levels of diversity and social mobility.[13]

> Point to Ponder
>
> Considering the above, what roadblocks have you erected or encountered, and how do you think these roadblocks affected your progress in life?
> If you overcame the roadblocks: how did you do that?
> If you are still struggling with the roadblocks, how do you plan to overcome them?

## Evaluating Setbacks

*Oprah Winfrey is one of the most famous African American women in the world, and one of the richest. Yet, this was not always the case. Born in Mississippi to a teen mother, she endured a turbulent youth marked by abuse, poverty, and living instability. She was first sent to her grandmother, then to her father, followed by a return to her mother, only to be sent back to her father. Her life story yields an early youth pregnancy leading to a premature birth of a son who died in infancy. But Oprah had one major strength: she was eloquent, and soon found her way to the media, where she moved up, even though she also regularly encountered harsh criticism and sometimes even rejection. She was plagued by low self-esteem, which manifested itself in her choices of partners in early adulthood: she needed approval and was willing to do almost anything to get that from the men in her life. She even toyed with the thought of suicide at some point, but luckily found the strength to veer away from that intent. Oprah's gritty outlook on life, and her ability to self-heal by freely allowing her emo-*

---

[13] White, L.T. (Jun 11 2019). Is Implicit Bias a Product of the Person or the Situation? *Psychology Today*. Retrieved from https://www.psychologytoday.com/us/blog/culture-conscious/201906/is-implicit-bias-product-the-person-or-the-situation

*tions to be displayed in her programs ultimately made her the strong icon she continues to be for many in this world.*[14]

Like so many of us, you have undoubtedly experienced the ups and downs of life's rollercoaster. And, like many of us, it's probably easier to talk about the ups than it is to mention the downs. Yet, before we even dive any further, keep in mind that you needed both, the ups and downs, to get to where you are now. So, let's park any feelings of reluctance and bashfulness, and face the facts. If you only consider the short excerpt of Oprah's story above, you can see that no one is spared from setbacks, because they are just as much a part of life as all other things. A setback is an event that gives you the feeling that you are losing progress as you experience delays from the goal you have formulated to accomplish.

In fact, we should be grateful for setbacks, because they give us the strength and resilience we would otherwise lack. And another important factor that we often overlook is that setbacks may sometimes just seem like that, but they could be blessings in disguise! One of the foundational thoughts of this book is that nothing happens without a reason. The only problem is that we cannot always see the purpose behind the things that happen to us. When we cannot see an immediate benefit, we simply label an occurrence as a setback, at least until we get to see the bigger picture. Perceived setbacks may happen to steer us away from a direction we are not supposed to go into.

Setbacks can come in many forms: through physical inability, lack of means to move ahead, lack of connections to help you accomplish your goal, shifting social conditions that change and derail your plans, legal problems that delay your ability to make progress, and many others. Even if you internalize that setbacks are ultimately important for your growth it's never fun to experience them, and they can take a tremendous toll on your self-esteem. If, for instance, you're in college working on a degree, and intended to do this in a quick timespan, you may experience a delay due to a parent's or sibling's illness as a setback. Even though there is little to do about it, it still holds you back, and may result in a longer timespan before reaching your goal.

Here are three things you should consider when you encounter a setback:

1. *Refrain from blaming yourself or others.*

Placing blame on anyone has never proven beneficial or constructive. It's a very reactive approach that places you in a victimized position, and once you

---

[14] Adopted from Oprah's biography as described in the Britannica and Wikipedia online encyclopedias.

allow yourself there, it can be hard to rekindle your self-esteem and drive. When you blame others for everything that happens, you display an external locus of control. That means that you are not responsible for anything in your life, and that is unrealistic and comes across as weak and unreliable. The opposite of an external locus of control is an internal locus of control, where you take responsibility for your actions. Entrepreneurs are known to have an internal locus of control: they are self-starters and don't blame anyone if things don't work out as expected.

In his book "Good to Great" Jim Collins[15] refers to this as looking in the mirror versus looking outside the window. He recommends looking in the mirror when things don't go well, and first take responsibility. When things go well, look outside the window, and praise those involved. That always makes a strong impression and attracts people to want to work with you.

So, when things don't go well, consider what happened, question why or how this happened, and see what you can do about it. It's also a great idea to keep the serenity prayer in mind: *"Grant me the serenity to accept the things I cannot change, the courage to change the things I can, and the wisdom to know the difference"*.

If you can change the situation, consider carefully whether this is wise and desirable. Remember, sometimes a setback occurs because you were not on the right path to begin with; sometimes it occurs because you may need to take pause and rethink potential unforeseen hurdles; and sometimes it just happens to test your perseverance and grit. Grit is the ability to proceed when the going gets though.

2. *Identify a source of insight*

Since you don't have all the knowledge in the world, there are always things that others could teach you. When you experience a setback in your goal, you may need some extra encouragement. Consider what the most prudent option might be given the path you are treading.

– Do you need to identify a mentor, who has the wisdom, experience, and insight to listen and possibly provide advice on next steps? Know that your mentor doesn't have to be a person active in the same field you're in. Sometimes it may be more refreshing, and leading to greater insights if you find a mentor who is insightful but doesn't know much about your field.

---

[15] Collins, J. (2001). *Good To Great: Why Some Companies Make the Leap and Others Don't*. HarperCollins Publishers, New York, NY.

This is when you will get outside-the-box feedback that can lead to innovative outcomes.
- Do you need to do some self-searching to see whether you truly are on the right path? Consider the option offered in chapter two about vipassana meditation. It is a marvelous technique to get you refocused.
- Do you need to do some research about the topic to find out if there are unexpected blind spots you need to clear? In that case you're definitely in luck, because the Internet offers so many options to learn about anything.

You may very well find that, once you have taken a break from the incessant process of heading in one particular direction, you can restart with renewed energy, deeper insights, and a more precise goal, possibly even with a slightly changed focus.

3. *Celebrate the opportunity*

You may wonder what there is to celebrate in the occurrence of a setback? Well, as mentioned earlier, everything happens for a reason. You needed the delay to refocus, and in the future there will definitely be an "aha!" moment when you realize what the reason was for the setback. Meanwhile, you should celebrate the learning moment that is embedded in any setback. Setbacks make you stronger, and they deepen your insight in all that can go wrong. I have heard setbacks being described as delayed success. I tend to agree, as long as you take the time to analyze what went wrong and what you can learn from the process. Think of Edison, who refused to see his unsuccessful efforts as failures, but considered them learning moments. We can all adopt this mentality.

> **Point to Ponder**
>
> Considering the above, think of a setback you encountered that really disturbed you when it happened.
> Did you identify a source of insight? What choice did you make?
> Looking back at the setback now: what can you celebrate about it?
> Is there any advantage you can identify at this stage related to the setback?

## Chapter Highlights

- *There is no victory in hanging your head when a load of life's lemons hits you.* Tapping into your inner sweets to convert the lemons into lemonade is a skill that you can learn. You can learn how to shift your lenses and start looking at the new situation from a variety of angles until you discover a way to cope with it, and hopefully even transform it into a blessing.
- *Three common mental roadblocks* we erect as we go through our daily routines are:

  1. Sleepwalking: When you go through your days without ever taking a moment to reflect on your circumstances, your behavior, the things you discussed, the decisions you made, their outcomes, and whether your life as it currently runs is really how you would like it, you are sleepwalking. Take a few minutes, possibly at the end of your day, to reflect on the things that went on and how you felt about them, you might surprise yourself in future actions and behaviors.
  2. Comfort Zone Clinging: We are creatures of habit and don't like change, especially not when it comes to major parts of our lives such as home, work, or any other routine we have become accustomed to. There is no key advice to be given here, because breaking away from what you are used to is just not easy. A leap in the dark sounds scary enough. The only thing that may help is caution. You can try to shine some light on the darkness you are supposed to leap into by exploring first.
  3. Implicit Biases: Implicit bias often leads to quick labeling of a large group of people based on one encounter or the behavior of one person. People who judge others on basis of implicit biases deprive themselves from some great opportunities to enlarge their horizons and work with a more diverse group of people. They thereby also limit their prospects to become privy of other insights that could be valuable in future situations.

- *Evaluating Setbacks*: keep in mind that you needed both, the ups and downs, to get to where you are now. We should be grateful for setbacks, because they give us the strength and resilience we would otherwise lack.
- *Three things you should consider when you encounter a setback*:

  1. Refrain from blaming yourself or others: Placing blame on anyone has never proven beneficial or constructive.
  2. Identify a source of insight: there are always things that others could teach you.
  3. Celebrate the opportunity: everything happens for a reason.

# 2

# Breathing = Life (and So Much More)

**Contents**

| | |
|---|---|
| The Essence of Breathing | 19 |
| Vipassana Meditation | 20 |
| Insights from Breathing | 25 |
| Chapter Highlights | 28 |

**Abstract** This chapter takes a closer look into the foundations of insight meditation (Vipassana), specifically the importance of the breathing exercise, and how this can serve as a constant reminder of the arising and passing nature of everything, similar to our inhales and exhales. It will entail an overview of the benefits this practice has brought to people in hopeless positions, such as convicted criminals in prison, who then discovered a new way of looking at life, and shifted their mindsets.

**Breathe Your Way to Calmness: A Story**
*Amongst the hundreds of birds in a luscious garden was one small bird, who was plagued by chronic anxiety. He had witnessed several of his buddies being abducted by the wide range of local predators, especially the cats, eagles, foxes, and coyotes. This small bird was so anxious that she spent almost all day in a large honey suckle bush to protect herself from harm.*

*When asked why she wasn't joining all the other birds who were enjoying the sun and all the seeds from the rich vegetation in the garden, she would tweet that she was afraid of dying.*

*Two birds, who felt sorry for their fearful friend, decided to take her under their wings and tell her about the essence of life. They tweeted that silent breathing and considering that everything arises and passes, just like your breath, can be a calming though and make you less disturbed and fearful of the daily challenges.*

*It took the two bird-tutors a few days to get the little bird to focus truly and intensely on her breath, but as she started practicing, the little bird felt calmer indeed, up to the point that she realized that it's no use to live in a panic all the time, because life is blessed as it is.*

*She finally decided to fully join her flock, and from then on, whenever she felt the old anxiety come up, she practiced some mindful breathing, and was able to resume feeding herself together with her friends.*

---

> Meditation is to be aware of every thought and of every feeling, never to say it is right or wrong, but just to watch it and move with it. In that watching, you begin to understand the whole movement of thought and feeling. And out of this awareness comes silence.[1]
>
> ~ *Jiddu Krishnamurti*

### Soothing

A peaceful home soothes
The weary mind
Like a gentle sanctuary
To finally unwind

Away from suspicions,
Incessantly brought forth
By spirits in search
Of their lost True North

No ranting oration
Just quietude here
No fuss or frustration
Nirvana is near

---

[1] https://www.brainyquote.com/quotes/jiddu_krishnamurti_752651

Away from all gloom
Is this blanket of calm
This peaceable room:
A therapeutic balm

As I quietly enjoy
This absence of strife
The clock ticks away
The times of my life

*–Joan Marques*

## The Essence of Breathing

You live because you breathe. Your breath signifies the difference between being alive or not. Yet, because we breathe continuously, even when we sleep, we take it for granted. How many of us take a moment when we sit behind the computer or stand in front of the fridge to say, "I'm so grateful that I breathe"? In fact, we only get frantic about our breath when we have trouble breathing, for instance, when we have a bad cold, or get an asthma attack, or deal with pressure on our chest. At any other time, we go our merry way, concentrate on the problems and jubilations of the day, and forget that we breathe.

Still, there is so much that we can learn from breathing. I once attended a Vipassana meditation retreat in India, and became acutely aware of the power of breathing. Your breath represents so much more than the inhaling and exhaling process through your nose. When you focus intensely on your breath you will discover that your nostrils alternate in the amount of airflow that goes through them. This is called the nasal cycle. About every two hours there is a shift whereby one nostril becomes slightly congested and the other decongests. Then, after a while, they alternate.

There is, however, another, even more important insight to consider. Your breath represents the reality of everything in life: arising and passing away, which I will dive into deeper in the next section about Vipassana. Yet, I think it's critical to keep in mind how much you can learn from your breathing, as it can keep you grounded when you find yourself fighting a little bit too hard for that position, or wanting to hold on just too long to that relationship. Your breath represents the cycle of life. Everything comes and goes: positions, possessions, honors, embarrassments, relationships, elations, devastations, and even your life. Nothing lasts. Everything arises and passes. Just like your breath.

## Vipassana Meditation

Meditation is not new: it has been around for millennia. And while some religions are big on meditation, the practice of meditation itself does not have to be religiously driven. Many people who meditate on a daily basis do so for their own mental and emotional stability, and not for religious purposes.

Today, workplaces have adopted meditation and silent rooms to allow employees time to center in the middle of their working day. They have found that it enhances personal balance within their employees, and increases calmness and acceptance amongst employees and between employees and external stakeholders.

With the expansion of information and tradition exchanges between East and West, we have seen practices moving around in the world, and meditation, including all the benefits it brings, is no exception to this trend. Meditation is often attributed to Buddhist practice, most likely because the man who is referred to as the "Buddha" (Siddhartha Gautama), found his valuable insights that eventually led to his teachings through the practice of vipassana meditation.

> History taught us that Siddhartha grew up in affluence, and knew of no concern until he was a young man. His father, a tribal leader, had ordered a strictly protective lifestyle for his son, because someone predicted shortly after Siddhartha's birth that he might become a great leader, a saint or an ascetic, the latter two not being in line with the father's plan. Yet, after many years of solid protection from the worldly influences, the young Siddhartha got out of his luxurious dwellings and witnessed illness, aging, and death amongst the people outside. This was the first time he saw anything other than young, healthy people, and it turned out to be a rude awakening. Siddhartha suddenly understood that he had been living in an unrealistic world. He decided to leave that all behind to search for the truth. For several years after leaving behind his lavish and protected life, he wandered from village to village, begging for food, and finally ended up living with a group of ascetics in the hills and the forests, hardly eating anything and depriving himself from almost everything. As the years went by, however, Siddhartha realized that neither of his extreme lifestyles, sheer abundance nor extreme abstinence, brought him any fulfillment. This is when he engaged in this vipassana meditative practice and arrived at the understanding that the middle path is the healthiest and most rewarding way to live.

Thanks to the ebb and flow of his breath, and the insights acquired through his meditation, Siddhartha, who was later renamed "the Buddha" realized that neither extreme side is healthy or satisfactory, while the middle path represents the balance we need to perform in a sustainably rewarding way.

Indeed, meditation has been around for many centuries, and the two forms of meditations that seemed to have bridged the longest span of time are Samatha or tranquility and Vipassana or insight meditation.

Samatha or tranquility meditation can provide your mind clarity and serenity. It prepares your mind to see things as they really are. Once that is the case, you have created the foundation for insight meditation. Vipassana meditation, then, is needed to acquire the insights that will help you see your path with clarity.

Vipassana meditation has gained increased popularity over the past decades, thanks to Satya Narayan Goenka,[2] an Indian businessman who personally experienced the benefits of this tradition and decided to pay it forward. Today, there are Vipassana centers in many parts of the world.

> The Vipassana website from Dhamma.org, the organization founded by S. N. Goenka underscores that the Buddha (Siddhartha Gautama) engaged in vipassana meditation to better understand the art of living. Vipassana can help us attain liberation from mental impurities and attain happiness. It is a practice that is very focused on the interrelatedness between body and mind with the aim to transform ourselves through self-observation. By doing vipassana, we become aware of our thoughts, feelings, judgements and sensations, and gain insight on how we contribute to our own suffering.

Goenka started teaching vipassana in 1969 and did so until he passed away in 2013. However, he set up a comprehensive training system so that future teachers could be trained and appointed to continue this useful tradition globally. The vipassana training is a ten-day exercise of serious devotion to the practice, whereby:

- The first agreement or step is to abstain from killing, stealing, sexual activity, speaking falsely, and taking intoxicants. The purpose of this moral agreement is to help calm the mind, as the above exercises just lead to anxiety and aggravation.
- The second step is to focus on the breathing process that flows through us constantly. This focus leads to increased inner calmness and receptivity to the third step.
- The third step entails undertaking the practice of Vipassana, which entails the observation of our bodily sensations, understanding their nature, and developing the mental and emotional balance to accept them without reaction.

Vipassana is therefore best described as a mental training that helps us develop a healthy mind.

---

[2] Goenka, S. N. (2008). *Vipassana Meditation - Sattipatthana Course*. In Shri Satyanarayan Goenkaji (Ed.), Dhamma Sikhara. Himachal: S. N. Goenka.

Vipassana exercises are offered at no cost, as the intention is to keep this healing practice out of the commercial realm. The ten-day practice should be seen as an initiation in self-preservation and wellness for years to come. It's not an end onto itself, but a means toward a beneficial and longitudinally sustainable end.[3]

Vipassana meditation follows four steps:

1. Slow Scan, which entails the process of slowly moving your attention from the top of your head to the tip of your toes and back, preferably in as much detailed focus as possible. Examine, as you do this scan, each part of your body slowly and attentively, but without judgment.
2. Free Flow Sweep, which means that, after the slow scan, you sweep your attention upwards and downwards your body, and carefully observe the areas where you experience subtle sensations. At all times, you refrain from getting upset or excited, but you just observe with equanimity.
3. Spot Check, which entails that you quickly focus on any spot that you feel needs attention. These spots may vary from one sitting to another. The practice is to move back and forth. Try about 4 to5 spots checks and then return to the normal scan and sweep.
4. Penetrating and Piercing, which goes beyond the focus of the three above steps. At this point, you engage in an internal scan where you shift your attention internally. The penetrating and piercing practice is usually reserved for the more seasoned practitioners, and preferably conducted under guidance of an experienced practitioner.[4]

The absolute value of insight meditation is the awareness that everything arises and passes, just like the breath, which you keep observing. The law of impermanence becomes abundantly clear when you practice vipassana. It is therefore not surprising that Goenka, the man who successfully reintroduced vipassana to the world, considers this practice a great contributor to becoming a better human being, and generating a peaceful and harmonious atmosphere around yourself and others. Vipassana is a useful instrument toward higher consciousness in people from all walks of life, and all parts of the world, especially because it is focused on your own inner balance, and not on a religious prescription.

---

[3] Vipassana Meditation as Taught by S. N., Goenka (ND). *Dhamma.org*. Retrieved from https://www.dhamma.org/en/about/vipassana
[4] Marques, J., & Dhiman, S. (2009). Vipassana meditation as a path toward improved management practices. *Journal of Global Business Issues, 3*(2), 77–84.

The insights you obtain through vipassana meditation are multiple and valuable. The increased awareness of the passing nature of everything this practice brings also makes you understand how futile it is to excessively cling to anything, since nothing lasts anyway. It also helps to understand the many rebirths you go through in this very life, as you constantly change, and therefore have the ability to shift your behaviors, practices, and insights. This means that, through the elevated awareness you acquire from vipassana, you realize that you can release old, limiting mental and behavioral patterns, and gravitate to those that embrace the idea of oneness amongst all living beings.

Insight meditation is a powerful tool, as you may have gathered from the brief explanation above. Because you observe the way things really are, and realize the passing nature of everything, you also become more receptive to other beings—human and non-human. Your respect for all that lives alongside you in this universe gets enlarged, and your approach to many things will change. You will release thoughts and practices of violence, because you understand how destructive this is to the overarching cycle of existence to which we are all part, your elevated consciousness realizes that actions such as killing, stealing, rape, and other wrongdoings come forth from destructive mindsets, which you can now recognize and abstain from. Through vipassana meditation you can break the habit pattern of your mind to generate destructions at its root level.[5]

Vipassana has been applied in prisons over the past decades. In India, there are several prisons that have a steady set of 10-day vipassana retreats for prisoners who are interested, and now there are also options for a limited groups of prisoners in the US and Canada. It seems that vipassana meditation can help improve many disorders such as alcohol and substance abuse, personality disorders, and literacy and learning disabilities, while it can reduce Post-Traumatic Stress (PTSD) symptoms and reduce senses of distrust and doubt within its practitioners.[6]

An experiment was conducted to test the value of using Vipassana meditation as a coping mechanism in prison. Vipassana course completers had a significantly better outcome than the comparison group, including reductions in drug use, anxiety, depression, and hostility.

---

[5] Marques, J., & Dhiman, S. (2009). Vipassana meditation as a path toward improved management practices. *Journal of Global Business Issues, 3*(2), 77–84.
[6] Zoukis, C. (Oct. 30, 2014). Vipassana Meditation Courses for Correction Facilities. Retrieved from https://federalcriminaldefenseattorney.com/vipassana-meditation-courses-for-correction-facilities/

*A great testimonial to the above is an essay written by a 45-year-old inmate, who participated in the meditation practices. Mark French, who at the time of writing the article was serving time in the Deer Lodge Correctional Facility, Montana, shares about the calmness he finally found in prison by reading Zen books and doing vipassana. He expressed great respect for Zen master Thich Nhat Hanh and his monastery in Plum Village, France, where, as he found out through his readings, a Vietnam combat veteran, just like him, found peace of mind.*

*French shares how the meditation practice started: with a very small group that slowly started growing. The sessions only lasted for 20 minutes, but they helped him face each day with a better outlook than before. French mentioned the mindfulness that he allowed in his life through his meditation practice, and how living in the moment is truly the only way to do prison time in peace.*

*The son of a Baptist minister, French shared his turbulent youth, and his pleasant surprise that it took this prison sentence for him to finally find the spiritual peace and wholeness he lacked before in his life. He praised the Buddhist community for caring enough for prisoners to assist them in finding peace and solace, and to even consider engaging in service projects to help others who suffer outside. And while freedom was still far away from Mr. French as he wrote his essay, he confessed that he could always turn to his breathing exercises, and his calming practice, which 'doing time' so much easier.*[7]

*In another essay, French shares his experience in solitary confinement, a "punishment" every inmate dreads with a passion. Those of us who have seen Papillon have witnessed how terrible this confinement period can be. Not for French, though. In this restrictive environment, referred to as "The Hole", French decided to treat himself to his own solitary mindfulness retreat. After a first day of being bummed by the foresight of this seemingly eternal time of solitude, French pulled himself together. He drew a Buddha, and created a daily routine with his cell becoming his own private meditation hall. Drawing from the readings he had done before, his day consisted of sitting and walking meditation alternations and study periods. When the 18 days of solitary confinement were over, French felt grateful for the opportunity to experience mindfulness and living in the moment more intensely that ever before.*[8]

*I now view this experience not as a punishment, but as an opportunity to learn first-hand what life in a monastery might be like. It was, indeed, a treat. I can't say I haven't agonized over the backward steps I've taken, nor have I avoided thinking about what the future holds. But I am fortunate to have a renewed outlook on mindfulness and living in the moment.*

---

[7] French, M. (March 1996). Being Present in Prison. *The Mindfulness Bell, 16*. Retrieved from https://www.parallax.org/mindfulnessbell/article/being-present-in-prison/

[8] French, M. (June 1996). Solitary Practice in "The Hole." *The Mindfulness Bell, 17*. Retrieved from https://www.parallax.org/mindfulnessbell/article/solitary-practice-in-the-hole/

> **Point to Ponder**
>
> Consider selecting a short (10–15 minutes) vipassana guided meditation from YouTube.
> Once completed, what were your most insightful and useful experiences? What were your concerns?

## Insights from Breathing

Here are some useful insights to consider about breathing:

1. *It reduces stress and enhances inner serenity.*

Focusing on your breath makes you aware of this very source of life you have. At the same time, it compels you to examine your breathing, and regulate it if you realize that you are agitated or nervous, and therefore breathing too fast. By observing your breath, you restore your inner calm, let go of external concerns, and become better able to rationalize matters.

2. *It resembles the impermanence of everything.*

As mentioned earlier in this chapter, your breath and its pattern of inhaling and exhaling resembles the impermanence of everything. Just like your breath entering and leaving your nose, so too does everything else arise and pass. By keeping this thought atop of your daily considerations, you will become better able to cope with change and letting go of familiar patterns that had become part of your daily routine. You may always remain a creature of habit, since you are human, but you will better understand and therefore accept the capricious twists of life and become better attuned into releasing old ways and accepting new ones.

3. *It quiets and sharpens the mind.*

Especially if you focus on your breath while meditating, you will find that concentrating on your breath calms the mind, and therefore sharpens its ability to reason. Sitting in a contemplative position and focusing on your breath can lead to insights you did not consider before. A calm mind gets the opportunity to flourish and become a conduit for innovative thoughts that would not have found their way through a cluttered, restless mind. Once the space for innovative thoughts has been created, you can cultivate the thoughts and explore their viability.

4. *It enhances your inner sense of gratitude.*

While this may initially come across as strange, it makes perfect sense if you think about it. Focusing on your breath makes you realize that you are alive and will therefore elevate your respect for *being able* to enjoy life. This sense of gratitude for life will also make you appreciate life for others as well, so you will become more mindful in your approach to others, human and non-human.

5. *It elevates your awareness of oneness with all living beings.*

Focusing on your breath and appreciating the gift of breathing also enhances your understanding that all that lives breathes in some way, shape or form. In humans and animals, it is more apparent, but plants breathe in their own way. By internalizing the awareness of you not being all that different from any other living being, you will acquire a deeper understanding of the overarching interdependency we all have toward one another, and you will be more apt to appreciate and respect all other forms of life (Fig. 2.1).

> Point to Ponder
>
> Focus for a few minutes in silence on your breath.
> Now, consider the above insights from breathing and rank the five insights in order of their appeal to you, starting with the highest appeal.
> Could you also come up with one or two additional insights from breathing?

### A Peaceful Home

A peaceful home soothes
The weary mind
Like a gentle sanctuary
To finally unwind

## 2 Breathing = Life (and So Much More)

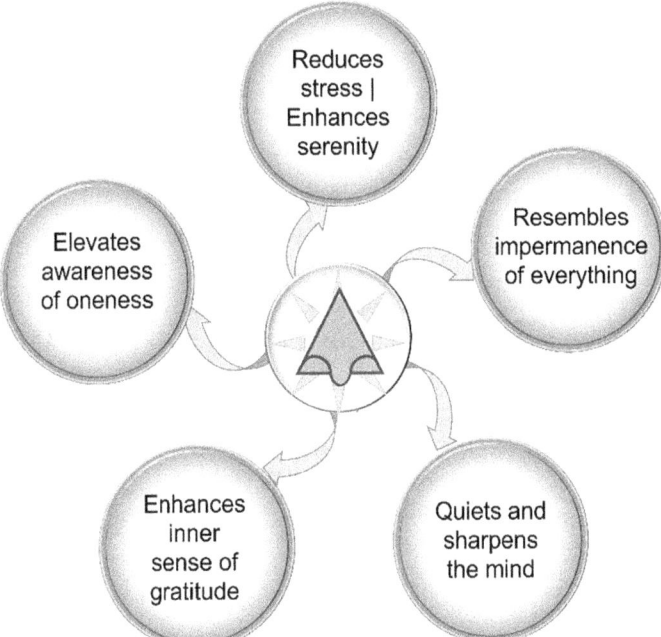

**Fig. 2.1** Insights from breathing

Away from suspicions,
Incessantly brought forth
By spirits in search
Of their lost True North

No ranting oration
Just quietude here
No fuss or frustration
Nirvana is near

Away from all gloom
Is this blanket of calm
This peaceable room:
A therapeutic balm

As I quietly enjoy
This absence of strife
The clock ticks away
The times of my life

*-Joan Marques*

## Chapter Highlights

- *The Essence of Breathing*: Your breath makes the difference between being alive or not. Your breath also represents the reality of everything in life: arising and passing away. It represents the cycle of life: everything comes and goes: positions, possessions, honors, embarrassments, relationships, elations, devastations, and even your life. Nothing lasts. Everything arises and passes. Just like your breath.
- *Vipassana Meditation*: This meditation technique has been around for millennia. The two forms of meditations that seemed to have bridged the longest span of time are Samatha or Tranquility and Vipassana or Insight meditation. The insights you obtain through vipassana meditation are multiple and valuable.
- *Insights from Breathing*: (1) It reduces stress and enhances inner serenity. (2) It resembles the impermanence of everything. (3) It quiets and sharpens the mind. (4) It enhances your inner sense of gratitude. (5) It elevates your awareness of oneness with all living beings.

# 3

# Life Is All GAIN

**Contents**

| | |
|---|---|
| The Fascinating Puzzle Called Life | 31 |
| Using Difficult Times to Your Advantage | 36 |
| GAIN Explained | 37 |
| Chapter Highlights | 39 |

**Abstract** In this chapter the most important message is that nothing in life is ever lost. Even if you cannot see the benefits of things that happen to you at any given moment, you will realize in the long run why they had to happen. It could be to free you up for a better opportunity in the future, to gain better insights in upcoming situations, or to re-examine the choices you make. At any rate: every experience brings a new awareness, just like a teacher who presents you with a lesson and then disappears to make place for the next one. In this chapter the GAIN-cycle is introduced, with an overview of the next four chapters, which will further explain the cycle.

**The World Is Your Reflection: A Story**
A young traveler had been on his way for several days when he saw a town in the distance. With renewed energy he walked toward the town, when he encountered an old man fishing in a lake nearby. He walked up to the old men and asked him if he was familiar with the people in this town.
  "Oh yes, said the man. Very much so!".
  "Well, can you tell me then how these people are?"

The old man replied, "First tell me where you came from and how the people were in that town."

"Oh, they were mean, shortsighted, and unfriendly!", answered the young man. "I did not like them at all and was glad when I could move on".

"Well," answered the old man, "These people are even worse! It's better you just move on!"

So, the young man continued his way.

Several days later, another young man who had been on his way for several days saw the same town in a distance.

With renewed energy he walked toward the town, when he encountered the same old man fishing in a lake nearby. He walked up to the old men and asked him if he was familiar with the people in this town.

"Oh yes, said the man. Very much so!".

"Well, can you tell me then how these people are?"

The old man replied, "First tell me where you came from and how the people were in that town."

"Oh, they were fantastic, helpful, and a lot of fun!", answered the young man. "I only left because I want to see some more of the world, but we had a great time while it lasted!".

"Well," answered the old man, "These people are even nicer! Go, and you'll find out yourself!"

So, the young man entered the town and had a great time.

---

> Meditation is to be aware of every thought and of every feeling, never to say it is right or wrong, but just to watch it and move with it. In that watching, you begin to understand the whole movement of thought and feeling. And out of this awareness comes silence.[1]
>
> ~ Jiddu Krishnamurti

**Times**

There are times
When my heart feels frozen
While my feet seem to be stuck
On hot coal

---

[1] https://www.brainyquote.com/quotes/jiddu_krishnamurti_752651

When the smile
That lights up my face
Is in absolute stark contrast
With my soul

When the days
Arduously twine together
As rusty strings
On a chain

And the sun,
In spite of all its brightness,
Yields the same effect
As the rain

When wisdom
And spiritual reasoning
Bring very little relief
To my mood

And I have to
Do my upper-level best
To keep in mind that
Life is good

*–Joan Marques*

## The Fascinating Puzzle Called Life

It took me a long time to realize that life is a fascinating puzzle, and that the art of living is to understand that you may not have all the pieces of your puzzle in your hand now, but you will receive them when the time is right. How I arrived at that understanding? By sheer reflection! But once I grasped this concept, it seemed that so many things started making sense.

> *In my twenties I had a fabulous career in mass-media: I was presenting daily radio programs and several recurring television shows, while running a successful advertising and PR company. I had no intention to change that. I was well-known and had more work than I could handle. I liked what I did, and was making good money too, so there was no reason to think that I would want to change directions any time soon. Aside from my media and PR work, I was also involved in a number of other entrepreneurial ventures with my then-partner, including a livestock farm,*

*a restaurant, a seafood import-export company, and a large seaworthy fishing boat with crew. Yet, in spite of this hectic routine, I always felt that my excellent intellectual exploration had ended abruptly after high school, and that there was more for me to accomplish in that regard. Sadly, the single university in my home country was going through a turbulent phase with no solid consensus on the type of degrees to offer or the format in which these should be offered. So, my repeated visits to the university campus for information invariably ended in disappointment about the invitation to return next year and see whether there had been any appealing developments.*

*At some point I learned about the start of a new four-years program in Business Economics, organized by a private institution, and my sister-in-law and I decided to give it a try. Classes met one night a week and the pace was steep. It was a tough ride, being a mom of three and an entrepreneur running multiple businesses at barely 24 years old, but I persevered and am happy to say that, at the end of four demanding years, I was one of only seven who managed to finish the program. So, now, I had my successful business, my family, and a bachelor's equivalent degree I could be proud of, even though I had no intentions whatsoever of using it. I thought earning that degree was more for my personal gratification. After all, I was making great money doing what I loved to do.*

*Fast forward twelve years, and life had changed significantly. As I shifted into my thirties, I became aware that advertising was no longer my passion: I had started to perceive it as an ethical dilemma. No longer was I interested in persuading people to purchase goods and engage in services I wasn't willing to try myself. I wanted to engage in more serious things: educating people about the things that would really make a positive difference in their lives. So, I shifted to creating documentaries, and producing human interest interview programs. They were a lot more rewarding, but still, the passion I never thought I'd lose, was no longer there. I needed a new horizon and realized that staying in my beautiful but small homeland was not going to provide me that gratification.*

*It took me a couple of years considering what my options were, and I kept my eyes and ears open with a renewed curiosity. The US seemed like a good idea to start entirely anew without the baggage of my past, and after exploring multiple states, my choice ultimately fell on California. I did what I never thought I'd do: leave my precious, always sunny home country to embark on a completely insecure future. In my first months in California, I attended several information sessions at a variety of universities, and when I found the right one, I was utterly pleased to learn that my four-years degree in Business Economics was accredited and accepted as a Bachelor's equivalent degree, granting me a clear and immediate entry into a graduate program! It was then that I realized why I completed that program twelve years ago, at a time that I couldn't even fathom what it would ever be good for.*

The above example is just one of many reflective realizations that taught me to never question the directions of my life. There are still many instances when I wonder what certain steps or actions are good for, but I have learned to trust that the benefits will reveal themselves sooner or later.

The reason I started with this story is because I still frequently hear students, and even highly educated and seasoned colleagues complain that some things they went through were a complete waste of their time. When I hear that, all I can do is silently chuckle and think: "Not so! You will realize the benefits sooner or later." Sometimes I share my insights with them, and ask them to practice some patience, because nothing is ever lost, but at other times I sense that it might be better to stay quiet about it and allow life to work its course.

Now, it is important to understand that life will always have ups and downs, and some of the downs can be rough, even when you tell yourself that the advantages to your current challenges will surface in the future. We all wonder at times whether we are on the right track and whether we made the right choices. I am no exception to that. We, human beings, miss the ability to see in the future, and I guess that's a good thing, because we might not always like what we would see, and probably live in a sheer nightmare from day to day if we did. The one thing I have found to work when times are less rosy is to envision that it could always be worse, and that there are always some good sides to every experience.

> There are several ways to make the best of a bad situation, regardless of its magnitude. I came across an article that suggested five steps to deal with troubling circumstances:
>
> 1. Consider the future: everything passes, and so will the current challenge. Nothing lasts forever, and that goes for the current problem as well.
> 2. Consider what you can and cannot do. You're never completely helpless, and if you think things through, you might discover what you have in your power that you could use to improve the situation. Think sober and keep your anxiety and despair under control.
> 3. Keep your expectations low. This works well when you have to face an event that you dread. By not expecting anything extraordinary or interesting, you may get pleasantly surprised by whatever really transpires.
> 4. Don't get overzealous, especially when you're looking at a grim situation, such as a disruption in your work situation, for instance. Keep your head up, but don't get too involved or too excited. That can safeguard your internal balance.
> 5. Consider what you have in your life to be grateful about, especially when the current situation looks really grim. There's always something you can think about that will make you feel better. Concentrate on that. As a reverse situa-

tion, you can also consider how the current problem could have been worse, and be grateful that such is not the case.[2]

There are more practices you could consider, depending on the degree, size, and format of the problem you are facing. You could try some of the following:

- *Accepting the situation for what it is.* If you stop denying what's happening, you may retain a better grip on yourself, and your suffering may subside sooner.
- *Refraining from fighting for control,* especially if there is no way that you will win. The quicker you relax and observe, the quicker you will regain some peace of mind.
- *Keeping a positive mind,* even if the situation is not desirable. Maintain an attitude that you can be proud of in hindsight.
- *Changing your viewpoint.* I mentioned this one before, and will keep doing that. Sometimes, looking at a situation through a different psychological lens may shine an entirely different light on things, and suddenly the "bad" is not so bad anymore.
- *Calling on those you can rely on*: family, partners, friends, colleagues—you may find some decent support in ways that can help you deal with the situation better.
- *Practicing self-care.* Do something that positively influences you and gives you a break from the negative cloud you have been wallowing in. You should not underestimate the power of pampering yourself.
- *Discovering the lesson in what is going on.* This can be a truly enriching experience, because there are sometimes multiple lessons to detect from one single occurrence. And the lessons are strength-builders for life.
- *Being flexible.* You may have to change your plans based on the circumstances, and while this is not always desirable, it could be a life saver, and a solid way to restore your self-confidence and outlook on life.
- *Practicing mindfulness.* Staying alert and focused is an important way of remaining calm and composed. Remember, meditation is a great way to accomplish that.[3]

---

[2] Gilbertson, T. (Feb. 16, 2021). How to Make the Best of a Bad Situation: 5 steps to a better mindset and a better outcome. *Psychology Today.* Retrieved from https://www.psychologytoday.com/us/blog/constructive-wallowing/202102/how-make-the-best-bad-situation

[3] Adopted and modified from Doubek, A. (2023). 21 Ways to Make the Best of a Bad Situation. *Dancing Through the Rain.* Retrieved from https://dancingthroughtherain.com/make-the-best-of-a-bad-situation/

> **Point to Ponder**
>
> Consider a challenge you are dealing with now.
> List three downsides and three upsides to the situation.
> Keep in mind that this may not be an easy task, but at least it will distract your mind from only focusing on the negativity of your current situation and probe some lighter notes to consider.

**Smaller Cycles**

The time between
Getting dressed in the morning
And undressed in the evening
Is shrinking

My mailbox
Is in fast forward mode
Contents get obsolete
While I am still thinking

The space between my showers
The distance between meals
And the intake of daily vitamins
Is melting away

My cycles are becoming smaller
As my years in life increase
Tomorrow is here
While I am still digesting today

As days become months
And months become years
Strife is superseded
By the will to retire

Life is a dash
From birth to death
Holistic view enters
As we slowly expire

*– Joan Marques*

# Using Difficult Times to Your Advantage

There are always some good sides to every experience. While this is true, it doesn't mean that you should dwell on situations that are demoralizing and negatively affect your outlook on life. Perhaps the best way to explain this is from a middle path perspective: no experience is wonderful 100 percent of the time, and no experience is dreadful 100 percent of the time. So, how can you decide whether to stay or go? You will need to assess whether the dreadful part overpowers the wonderful part or vice versa. Any experience that is, on average, more dreadful than fun, should ultimately be released. But, as mentioned earlier, that is not always as easy as it may seem. It often takes time to find the right alternative. Here's where you have to implement mindfulness: stay only as long as needed in an unrewarding situation, and start preparing for the next stage. Keep your eyes open for opportunities, as they will surely surface.

In the meantime, you should also remain mindful of the fact that every experience is a teacher. There is something to learn from the situation, and the sooner you do, the quicker the teacher will disappear. So, if you find yourself in a less desirable position, consider the lessons to be learned from it.

> *A few decades ago, I encountered a situation where one person in my work environment was being extremely unpleasant. This lady had been on the hiring committee that decided for me to be hired as a professional academic advisor. She had been vehemently against my hiring but was outnumbered by the other committee members. From that time on, she did not let any opportunity pass to make me feel that she did not approve of my being there. She would deliberately not answer if I talked to her—so I stopped doing that—and she would look the other way when we would come across one another in the hallways. Troubled by this behavior, I consulted with one of my mentors, who told me a story of 20 students in a classroom, 19 of whom were diligent and good learners, and one was a real problem. This person did not only disrupt the lessons, but also stole food from the others whenever he could. Needless to say that his classmates considered him a terrible nuisance. One day, the teacher had to leave, and the 19 "good" students used the opportunity to join forces and chase away the one they considered a bad apple. Yet, when the teacher returned, he inquired about the missing student and looked concerned when the others told him that they could now resume their learnings without any annoying distraction. To the 19 students' surprise, the teacher put on his hat and coat again the next day and left, only to return several days later with… the troublemaker.*
>
> *The 19 eager learners were disheartened and asked the teacher why he brought the troublemaker back. The teacher then spoke, "If he's not around, who will teach you perseverance, understanding, patience, resilience, and tolerance?"*

*This short story changed my perspective, and I realized that, in spite of all the great things that were happening at my workplace, I had been allowing one colleague to ruin my experience. I decided to not let that go on any longer. A few years after internalizing this lesson, I told my mentor that I had not seen this "difficult" colleague around for a while, and he told me with a chuckle that she had retired more than a year ago!*

*This experience helped me understand that my change of perspective literally reduced an initially perceived problem to something insignificant, making the experience no longer cumbersome, and improving my work experience tremendously.*

## GAIN Explained

When you decide to consider your not-so-pleasant experience a teacher from which you need to learn, you may find that:

— Taking a different stance toward the situation will help you realize that you may have been obsessing over one negative aspect and overlooking the many pleasant and rewarding parts of the experience. Alternatively, the very aspect you initially considered negative may transform into a promise for the future if you just consider it through a different lens. You may, for instance, consider being transferred to a department in a quieter area a disaster, until you learn that there are great opportunities for spending quality and relaxing time during weekends in this new location: something you always longed for but never experienced in the hectic city.
— Your observations in the current environment will help you identify red flags in future opportunities, which means that you will get a better idea of the things you need to avoid in oncoming circumstances. Think of how much time, effort, and frustration this insight might save you! Just keep in mind, however, that there are no perfect situations, and that there will always be challenges of some kind in any environment. In other words, don't think that you should wait until the perfect opportunity will arrive. There are plenty of wise statements that tell us that it will seem that it's never the right time to commence something you are passionate about. Those fears you will have to overcome, and you will have to use your healthy judgment, experience, and conscience, to decide when to engage in your new endeavor.
— You landed in the current situation for a reason. Try to discover that reason, internalize it, and then move on. Don't blame yourself for having made "the wrong choice", because staring at the past is like trying to open a

sealed door to which you no longer have the key. Philosophically seen, there are no wrong choices if everything happens for a reason. So, no matter how much you dread a current situation, the light of tomorrow will explain the purpose of today. The best you can do is look ahead, and know that this, too, shall pass. Just make sure it doesn't pass without some important take-aways that will reshape your path for the future.

In the next chapters, we will review the concept of GAIN, which stands for Generating, Appreciating, Internalizing, and Newness. Gain simply represents the cycles we go through in multiple areas of our life (work, relationships, school, social environments, and more) and in our life overall.

We will first examine the process of generating, in which we absorb an experience, and get confronted with its pleasant and concerning aspects.

We will next review the stage of appreciating, which will be explained in more detail, as it is understandable that not every moment will be as desirable as we would like to. Yet, that doesn't mean that we cannot appreciate it in the greater scheme of things (Fig. 3.1).

Following the appreciation section, we will deliberate about internalizing, which is the process of contemplating what we should learn and take away from the experience. Vipassana meditation may be a very useful practice herein.

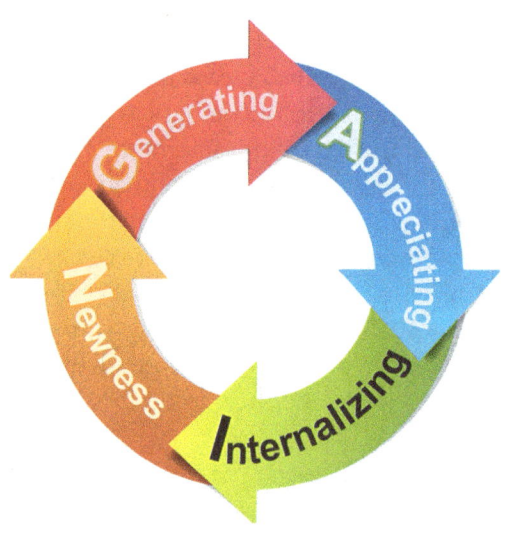

**Fig. 3.1** GAIN

Newness, finally, is the "rebirth" we experience when closing one chapter in our life and entering another. Every experience changes us, and invariably, we come out more seasoned, with greater insights, and overall, wiser.

## Chapter Highlights

- *Nothing in life is wasted*. You will realize the benefits in due time. We, human beings, miss the ability to see in the future, and that's a good thing, because we might not always like what we would see.
- *Use Difficult Times to Your Advantage*: There are always some good sides to every experience. Remain mindful of the fact that every experience is a teacher. There is something to learn from the situation, and the sooner you do, the quicker the teacher will disappear.
- *There are several ways to make the best of a bad situation*, regardless of its magnitude. Based on the nature of the situation, you can work on a range of ways to make matters better.
- *Take a different stance toward a situation*: This may help you realize that you may have been obsessing over one negative aspect and overlooking the many pleasant and rewarding parts of the experience. Your observations may help you define red flags in future opportunities, which means that you will get a better idea of the things you need to avoid in future circumstances.
- *You landed in the current situation for a reason*. Try to discover that reason, internalize it, and then move on.
- *Look ahead, and know that this, too, shall pass*. Just make sure it doesn't pass without some important takeaways that will reshape your path for the future.
- *Newness is the "rebirth" you experience*. This happens when you close one chapter in your life and enter another. No matter how much you dread a current situation, the light of tomorrow will explain the purpose of today.

# 4

# Generating: The Experiences Life Presents Us

## Contents

Connecting the Dots.................................................................................................... 42
Generating: Elements to Cultivate................................................................................ 45
Chapter Highlights...................................................................................................... 51

**Abstract** This chapter is the first in the GAIN cycle. It explains the notion of Generating. It will invite you to consider every experience as a generated piece of the puzzle that is your life, only to fit perfectly in the greater scheme of things in due time. It will further elaborate on the perception of experiences as teachers, not all of whom you will appreciate at first sight, but all of whom have an important lesson to teach us in the end. Concepts of patience, acceptance, forgiveness, and grit (perseverance) will be critical in this chapter.

### The Old Owl's Insights: A Story

Deep in a forest lived an old owl. Some of the animals claimed that he was 200 years old, but maybe that was just because he was so wise.

The old owl often sat quietly on his favorite branch in the Hyperion, one of the tallest trees around. Most of the time he was sleeping… or so it seemed.

One day a young owl approached the old fella and asked him what, based on his vast experience, his most precious lesson in life was.

The old owl uttered a deep sigh and then answered:

> I have come to understand that every experience is valuable in the end. Everything I have gone through so far has turned out to add a beautiful adornment to the patch-blanket that is my life.

> Some experiences were dark, others bright, but together they created a fabulous mosaic of which I would not change one piece.

Just as suddenly as he had started to speak, the old owl stopped talking and dozed off again… or so it seemed.

The young owl thought for a while and then intended to keep this advice in mind from here onward.

---

> The purpose of life is to live it, to taste experience to the utmost, to reach out eagerly and without fear for newer and richer experience.[1]
> ~ *Eleanor Roosevelt*

## Connecting the Dots

Steve jobs, the former CEO of Apple, referred to the use of life's experiences as connecting the dots. He was convinced that everything has a purpose, and that the future will reveal how past experiences fit in the wholeness of your life.

In this book, I refer to the sequence of experiences as *generating*. Whether you are aware of it or not, and whether it is your intention or not, you are constantly generating new dots to connect in the future. I believe that this in and of itself is a powerful paradigm. It can help you refrain from seeing anything as wasted time.

As I indicated before, there will never be a 100 percent satisfaction rate on any day, in any job, relationship, or experience. This may be the part where generating sounds somewhat debatable, because no one wants to generate dull, boring, or even aggravating experiences. Still, just like every 24-hour cycle consists of day and night, so too will the generating process of experiences consist of great and not-so-great moments: some we consider light, and others we consider dark. There is, however, always something to learn from them, and they will always contribute to your future.

> *Arnold Schwarzenegger is as good an example as any when we discuss the power of generating. As a poor Austrian youngster, he was dreaming of moving to the US, where there were so many opportunities. Indeed: wanting to end in America as a successful person became the vision around which he operated ever since his early high school years. He started weightlifting and body building exercises in his early*

---

[1] https://iperceptive.com/authors/eleanor_roosevelt_quotes.html

*teens, inspired by Reg Park, an English bodybuilder, businessman and actor. At age 19 he had an opportunity to meet Mr. Park, who promptly became his mentor, inspiring the young man to invest all the time and effort he could in realizing his dream. It paid off, and Arnold started winning contests, eventually moving to the US to explore bigger and better opportunities. Eventually his hard work was awarded by repeated Mr. Europe, Mr. Olympia, and Mr. Universe wins.*

*As he next aspired a career as an actor, he used his muscular body as the ticket to acquiring his first role, and from there he moved up to become one of the most famous actors in the 1990s. It required speech lessons to get rid of his thick Austrian accent, and while the accent never entirely subsided, he made great strides in ascending into celebrity status.*

*His next interest was politics, and again Arnold reinvented himself through learning, communicating, and promoting himself and became a two-time governor of California. Then, once retired from politics, he returned to acting, while he also invested in several business ventures. Arnold's story is and inspiring one revealing a chain of successes.*[2]

*And yes, Schwarzenegger has made his share of mistakes, most infamously, fathering a child with the family housekeeper, even though one could refute whether anyone's birth into this world should be considered a mistake. To clarify, it is not the birth of an innocent child that is the mistake, but the act of infidelity toward one's partner by engaging in a physical relationship with a third party, most disturbingly, and employee in the family household.*

*Yet, overall, we can extract quite some inspiration from Mr. Schwarzenegger's professional path, which made several turns, required multiple reinventions, and expanded his horizon in many constructive ways.*

In considering the most prominent dots in Schwarzenegger's life, it becomes obvious that his hard work as a bodybuilder served as the foundation for his future successes. Little could he have known that this practice would also become his ticket to the big screen, which, in turn, would grant him the celebrity status to become a successful politician. Arnold clearly took every experience as a teacher toward the next journey in his life and became rather good at doing so. And while, as is usually the case with celebrities and anyone else, not everyone likes him, we could all conjure some respect for his accomplishments as an immigrant in a world where making it so big is a true feat of perseverance.

*Suzanne Watson's name may not ring as loud a bell as Arnold's, but her story of generating and using her experiences as teachers may be even more inspiring. Suzanne*

---

[2] Schwarzenegger, A. (2019). *Arnold Schwarzenegger Leaves the Audience SPEECHLESS | One of the Best Motivational Speeches Ever*. Retrieved from https://www.youtube.com/watch?v=1bumPyvzCyo

*managed to become a medical doctor 25 years after initially being accepted to medical school. Life had a series of plans for her, none of which she may have anticipated. At the time she got accepted to Medical School as a young woman, she had a baby of less than one year old and another on the way, and she dropped out of the program within a week, realizing that this was not the right time.*

*Married life brought her four children and kindled an interest in the ministry. Suzanne became a priest, right at the time that her husband, who had a good position at a local hospital, committed suicide, most likely to avoid the stigma that would arise from reaching out for help with his mental issues The family fell on hard times, and Suzanne and her children had to adjust their lifestyle. She embarked upon her profession as a priest and raised her children, but never forgot about her vision of becoming a physician.*

*As she approached 50 and the kids had grown up, her oldest son encouraged her to rekindle her medical path. At first, she was inhibited, especially when seeing how much younger her follow students were. Fortunately, Suzanne did not let this deter her from going for her wish, and soon found that she had one great advantage over her younger peers: having been a mom raising kids had enabled her to be grittier and more perseverant in accomplishing her goals, even if that meant making sleep optional.*[3]

*While maintaining her career as a priest, Suzanne specialized in family medicine and psychiatry, and first moved to Nevada as a resident physician, and then to San Diego, California, where she became a psychiatrist in a local psychiatric clinic.*[4]

In considering the most prominent dots in Suzanne Watson's life, we detect an inspirational return to a long-cherished vision, that laid dormant during the years where accomplishing it was simply an impossibility. This did not mean that Suzanne sat idly while dealing with the capriciousness of life and family. She reinvented herself and embarked upon a career that was gratifying and through which she made a difference in the lives of those she encountered. This was also a career, however, that enabled her—timewise—to raise her family while working. Yet, once that was accomplished, the initial vision returned in full force, and converting that into reality became the crown on her professional journey.

---

[3] The Washington Post (June 9, 2019). *Changing Channels*. Retrieved from https://www.washingtonpost.com/graphics/2019/lifestyle/women-over-50/

[4] Watson, S. (2023). *LinkedIn* Profile. Retrieved from https://www.linkedin.com/in/suzanne-watson-9736b38/

> **Point to Ponder**
>
> Reflect on your own professional life.
> What are, in your opinion, the most important experiential generations you acquired?
> How did these generated gems serve you in new endeavors?
> How can you see these gems be of use to you in the future?

## Generating: Elements to Cultivate

Now, let's consider some of the concepts Arnold and Suzanne encountered and used in the generating process. As Arnold clearly states in his YouTube speech[5]: you need a vision. Both people discussed in this chapter carried one, and held it as a beacon before their mind's eye, in spite of the many distractions they encountered.

Some other qualities we can detect are:

### Patience

Neither Arnold's nor Suzanne's path were short ones. Arnold had to invest many years of ruthless training to get a chance at going overseas to his envisioned destination, America. Suzanne had to shift directions entirely for several decades before the opportunity to make her dream come true resurfaced. While they may not have experienced those long preparatory years as a manifestation of patience, we can see in hindsight that they both had to put in hard work, practice, and waiting to seize the right moment to move into the finale of their vision accomplishment.

### Acceptance

The interpretation of acceptance is different for each of the two individuals discussed here. Schwarzenegger accepted every opportunity he received to move closer to his goal and did not allow distractions from his plan as a young man. For Suzanne, the acceptance was geared toward having to shift gears and directions for nearly three decades before refocusing on the initial plan.

---

[5] Schwarzenegger, A. (2019). *Arnold Schwarzenegger Leaves the Audience SPEECHLESS | One of the Best Motivational Speeches Ever*. Retrieved from https://www.youtube.com/watch?v=1bumPyvzCyo

## Forgiveness

This may seem like a misplaced topic, but there is a lot of forgiving we must do as we go through the generating process of life's experiences. As Arnold was making his way to the top, he had to forgive himself for not always winning, and had to come to terms with making sacrificing that undoubtedly stood in the way of the fun other young people were having while he was working out. In Suzanne's case, she had to forgive her husband for leaving her and the children to fend for themselves, even though she eventually understood what led to his act. Perhaps she also felt that she had to forgive herself for not being able to keep her husband from taking his own life.

## Grit

Both, Arnold and Suzanne are very gritty people. Grit cannot be taught. It's a natural tendency to bounce back and overcome impediments toward succeeding. The two discussed individuals in this chapter persevered in their vision and managed to reinvent themselves multiple times throughout their career. It took several returns to the mental drawing board for Arnold as he was shifting from one career to another, even though he successfully transferred the qualities that worked in one career to the next. Suzanne, on the other hand, had to develop an entire new passion that would enable her to raise her family as a working parent. She managed wonderfully, and demonstrated her gritty nature once again when she decided to return to medical school after the age of 50.

> **Point to Ponder**
>
> Between patience, acceptance, forgiveness and grit: please rank the quality you feel to be most strongly represented in you?
> Share an example how you were able to apply the selected strength?
> Now, consider the quality you need to work on.
> Share an example where you could have used this skill and did not?

Figure 4.1 above depicts the qualities you will need to take optimal advantage of the generating process. The different colors of the elements, which should not be seen as the only important elements in the generating process, reflect the intensity of each:

## 4 Generating: The Experiences Life Presents Us

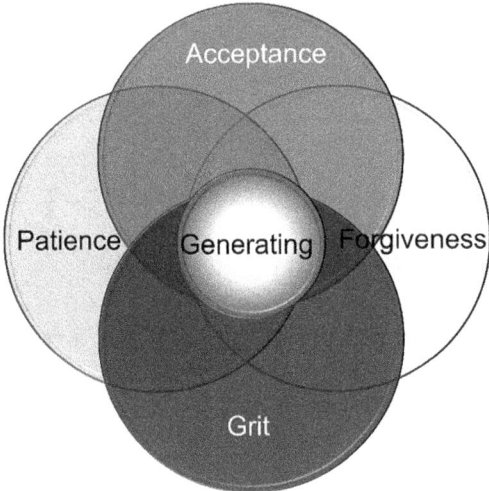

**Fig. 4.1** The process of generating

- Patience is a virtue, even though it is not always easy to practice. This explains the gray depiction. Patience is often disliked, especially if you are climbing the career ladder. The last thing you want to hear is that you should be patient. Yet, you wouldn't believe—unless you have experienced it—how easy it is to slide multiple ranks down that ladder by an unexpected situation. In practicing patience, you should consider multiple angles:

  - Keep your tendency to be impulsive under control: when you do hasteful things, you may regret the outcome. It's better to sleep one night over that email you want to send, or the call you want to make. You can prevent a lot of damage by being just a little bit more mindful.
  - Consider your reputation. Others have a certain impression of you, and it's good to be aware of that impression, so that you can either work on maintaining it—if it is what you want—or improve it. That takes time, but it's worth it.
  - Persevere where it's needed. Perseverance is the major difference between people who reach the top and those who don't. Don't walk away prematurely. Stick with something if you consider it good. In the end it will not only make others respect you more, but it will boost your self-confidence as well.

- Be grateful for the lessons in patience, as they will strengthen your backbone every time you experience something you perceive as a setback. This is how wisdom is born.[6]

— Acceptance is a skill that is sometimes easier to conjure than others, depending on what is at stake during the generating process. Because acceptance can be a fluctuating sense, it was represented in a darker gray. There are, however, multiple advantages to practicing acceptance.

- It will teach you the practice of humility. When you accept a situation, development, or practice, you first and foremost must surrender your own control. That is the very nature of accepting, and it can be a profound power and influence reducer.
- It will enhance your comfort with change. Accepting that something is no longer fulfilling to you (e.g., a job or a relationship) will give you the boost to work toward change. Without acceptance in this regard, there will be no action, and no new, more fulfilling reality.
- It will elevate your internal calmness, because you are fine with something that you may have initially rejected. Once you accept the situation, you release stress and suffering, and internalize emotional and physical health.
- It will also enhance your self-appreciation. If you learn to accept yourself, even in circumstances that are not in line with your plans, you cultivate an increased degree of serenity that can be critical for your wellbeing.
- It can help move things ahead. As long as you fight against a situation, you are delaying your own progress, and possibly the progress of others. Acceptance is therefore not only good for the maintenance of mutual respect and a pleasant environment, but also for the progression of the situation at hand.[7]

— Forgiveness is a hard practice sometimes, but it invariably leads to a clean conscience and a more balanced outlook than before once granted, whether that is to yourself or to others. It also leads to peace of mind.

---

[6] DeWind, R. (2023). The benefits of having patience. *Rochester Business Journal, 38*(32), 11.
[7] Fintzy Woods, R. (31 Aug. 2018). 14 Benefits of Practicing Acceptance. *Psych Central*. Retrieved from https://psychcentral.com/blog/cultivating-contentment/2018/08/14-benefits-of-practicing-acceptance#1

The Harvard Medical school, describes the REACH method as a simple and easy to memorize way of forgiving others. The authors of this work rightfully consider forgiveness important as it will free you from the damage of chronic inflammation, which can lead to a number of diseases such as cardiovascular disease, cancer, type 2 diabetes and more.

The article points out that there are two sides to forgiveness: decisional and emotional. Decisional forgiveness involves your deliberate choice to replace bad feelings toward someone with good ones. Emotional forgiveness is a more intricate process, whereby you no longer dwell on the foundation of the hurt that was caused. The REACH process, which can make this possible, consists of the following steps:

- **R**ecall the wrongdoing. Work toward no longer thinking of the offender as the foundation for your hurt. Analyze and try to understand the wrong that was done in a sober light.
- **E**mpathize. At this stage, you try to understand the reasons for the other party to cause the hurt. You may come to valuable insights there and realize that the goal may not have been to hurt or harm you per se.
- **A**ltruistic gift. At this stage, you reflect on your own instances of hurting others, and how you have been forgiven.
- **C**ommit. Make the forgiveness a real deal. If you can, write about it without sending your note to anyone. That makes it more solid for yourself. Commit yourself to forgive.
- **H**old on to the forgiveness. You may sometimes feel the anger and hurt flaring up again, and in those instances it's important to recall the REACH process, so that you can hold on firmly to the forgiveness for your own wellness.[8]

— Grit is a profoundly valuable quality but can be hard to conjure if you have not practiced it before. You are the only one who can teach yourself to become grittier, so it starts with an enormous dose of self-discipline. These are some practices to build grit:

- Identify your weak spots and start working on them. We have a tendency to turn a blind eye to our weaknesses, and only focus on our strengths. But our weaknesses can be a major impediment in persevering toward success. Be honest, pitiless, and strong in your evaluation, and if needed, ask those who know you best if they can help you identify your weaknesses.

---

[8] *The Power of Forgiveness* (Feb. 12. 2021). *Harvard Health Publishing: Mind and Mood.* Retrieved from https://www.health.harvard.edu/mind-and-mood/the-power-of-forgiveness

- Eliminate the distractions. This will require strictness. It is so easy to allow yourself to get on the social media channels again or play that game one more time, especially when you are bored or struggle with your project. Remove apps that you simply cannot leave alone, or limit your time to use these leisurely practices.
- Create new routines and habits of which you know they will enhance your success. Making lists of things to do and setting deadlines can be a great start in elevating your self-discipline.[9]

Since grit cannot be taught by others but needs to be mustered internally, it can be a tough ride, but it will be a rewarding one in the GAIN process of your life.

**A Fascinating Ride**

Aging is a fascinating ride
From assumed invincibility
To undeniable fragility

Riding…

On a road paved
With altering shades
Of awareness
Under an unpredictable sky –
Spanning from a vague sunrise
Through occasional rainbows
To an indisputable sunset

Marked by experience
Soft, shaded, or sharp
Crisp, cool, or cozy

Induced by
What we dreamed, dared, or did
Who we loved, loathed, or left
Within our bliss, bluff, or blast

---

[9] Get Grit: What Is Grit and How can it Benefit You? (ND). *Pace University Counseling Center.* Retrieved from https://www.pace.edu/counseling/resources/get-grit

# 4 Generating: The Experiences Life Presents Us

Floating…

On a cloud of impermanence
From invincibility
To fragility

*–Joan Marques*

## Chapter Highlights

- *Generating*: This is the sequence of experiences. You are constantly generating new "dots" to connect in the future. Just like every 24-hour cycle consists of day and night, so too will the generating process of experiences consist of great and not-so-great moments. There is always something to learn from them, and they will always contribute to your future.
- *Elements to Cultivate*:

    - *Vision*: keep your eye on the goals you have set for yourself.
    - *Patience*: put in hard work, practice, and wait to seize the right moment. Patience is a virtue, even though it is not always easy to practice. This explains the gray depiction.
    - *Acceptance*: This may pertain to accepting the opportunities to move closer to your goal, or accepting the other paths you need to explore before returning to your initial goal. Acceptance is a skill that is sometimes easier to conjure than others, depending on what is at stake during the generating process. Because acceptance can be a fluctuating sense, it was represented in a darker gray.
    - *Forgiveness*: There is always something to forgive, not only to yourself, but also to others around you. Forgiveness is a hard practice sometimes, but it invariably leads to a clean conscience and a more balanced outlook than before once granted, whether that is to yourself or to others. It also leads to peace of mind.
    - *Grit:* this cannot be taught. It's a natural tendency to bounce back and overcome impediments toward succeeding. Grit is a profoundly valuable quality but can be hard to conjure if you have not practiced it before. Since grit cannot be taught by others but needs to be mustered internally, it can be a tough ride, but it will be a rewarding one in the GAIN process of your life.

# 5

# Appreciating: Valuing the Experiences

**Contents**
Finding Light in Darkness............................................................................................... 54
Appreciating: Being the Light......................................................................................... 58
Chapter Highlights........................................................................................................... 65

**Abstract** This chapter focuses on the second aspect of GAIN: Appreciating. The chapter sympathizes with the general notion that not every situation is one to be celebrated. The many forms of losses we experience in life (death, lay-offs, bankruptcy, divorce, etc.) are hurtful and demand a long time to overcome. Yet, in every difficult situation we can also find some points of gratitude—for what was, for what we have learned, for how we grew, and for whatever still is to come. Change sometimes comes disguised as a curse and only later reveals its blessing. Concepts of reflection, suffering, perspectives, choice, and change will be important in this chapter.

**Observe, Learn, and Appreciate: A Story**
Near the foothills in the county lived a family of raccoons: a mother, a father, and a young son named Jasper. Through the day, the family stayed in their den in the mountains, and at night they made their rounds through a nearby neighborhood in search of food.

The smallest of the raccoons, Jasper, was fearful that someone may want to harm him, so he always hid in the bushes, and did not get much to eat.

The older raccoon decided to help little Jasper a hand and took him to a yard where a friendly family was always putting out tins with cookies for the raccoons every night. He told Jasper that it's good to be cautious, because not everyone was friendly. However, it's also good to explore your surroundings and find out who is worthy of your trust. Some people were, indeed, friendly and went out of their way to feed the local wildlife.

After several nightly trips to the same yard and always finding the cookie cans filled, Jasper realized that, truly, there were friendly souls in the world, indeed. You just had to observe, learn, and appreciate.

> The Happiest people do not necessarily have the best things. They simply appreciate the things they have.[1]
>
> ~ *Warren Buffett*

**As We Mature**

As we mature
We have to endure
More losses than before
Dear ones are suddenly no more
Yet, in spite of feeling stressed
We can choose to feel blessed
Remembering those we used to know
And how they helped us grow
As we slowly proceed on our way
In gratitude for yet another day

*-Joan Marques*

# Finding Light in Darkness

You may not be able to influence everything you experience, but you have the power to decide how to perceive it. Not everything you go through is worth celebrating, but it always contributes to your enrichment, the expansion of your horizon, and your future outlook on life.

---

[1] https://www.azquotes.com/quote/864511?ref=appreciate-life

## 5 Appreciating: Valuing the Experiences

Epictetus, a Greek stoic teacher who was born around AD 50 left us some strong and sensible quotes. The following I particularly appreciate:

*It's not what happens to you, but how you react to it that matters*[2].

Epictetus felt that all external occurrences are beyond our control, so we should simply accept them. However, he also felt that this did not justify lethargy or indolence, since we are still responsible for our actions. We should therefore behave with ultimate self-discipline.

Victor Frankl wrote something similar in his famous book, Man's Search for Meaning[3]:

*Everything can be taken from a man but one thing: the last of the human freedoms—to choose one's attitude in any given set of circumstances, to choose one's own way.*

The fact that Frankl's statement is phrased in a more dramatic tone than Epictetus' should be perceived against the backdrop in which it was made. Frankl was a Jewish psychotherapist, born in Austria, and taken to the infamous concentration camps during the Hitler's Nazi-regime. He spent three years in four camps, and survived by providing medical services, and by focusing on rewriting the book that had been taken away from him when he was imprisoned. He felt that creating a purpose would keep him alive, and this turned out to be true. His entire family including his young wife died in the camps, but he was released once the war was over, resumed his life and professional practice, got remarried, and lived to the age of 92.

The two statements here above underscore our human ability to interpret the things that happen to us in the ways we deem fit. This is an important piece of insight, because our interpretation of anything often depends on our mood at the moment. It is therefore important to reflect at the end of every day, and sometimes several days or weeks later, as our perspective may have mellowed and our interpretation balanced.

*Jan Ernst Matzeliger, born in Suriname out of a Surinamese mother and a Dutch father, left his home country at 19 to see more of the world. He arrived in the US in 1873, and had quite a hard time learning English and being accepted in Philadelphia, where he resided. He was a person of color in an era where double*

---

[2] https://www.brainyquote.com/quotes/epictetus_149126
[3] Frankl, V. (2006). *Man's Search for Meaning*. Beacon Press, Boston, MA.

*standards were still widely accepted. He found work in the shoe industry in a time where all shoes were still made by hand. Matzeliger began experimenting with the design of machines, ultimately developing a shoe lasting machine that could produce 700 pairs of shoes a day, which was more than 10 times the amount typically produced by human hands.[4] Matzeliger's invention mechanized the complex process of joining a shoe sole to its upper, and revolutionized the shoe industry He patented his invention, but it was later acquired by a shoe factory, as Matzeliger died from tuberculosis shortly after his invention. He was only 37, and his premature death could be attributed to neglecting his health as he worked long, exhausting hours on his invention and did not eat regularly.[5]*

*Matzeliger made a lasting impression on human reality, demonstrating that a practice that had been completed manually for many centuries before, could be done with a machine, thereby increasing output immensely. His situation had not been easy, and he did not have a long life, but chose to make a positive contribution and to give his life and legacy a timeless purpose. Based on his story Matzeliger embodied the ability to reflect on what truly mattered in life and converted the suffering he undoubtedly experienced as an immigrant of color in a predominantly White community to virtue. He knew he had the choice between remaining a nobody or making a difference, and he chose the latter, even though he was deliberately left out of the history books because of the color of his skin. It took a very long time before Matzeliger received some posthumous recognition for his machine, which is still considered the greatest forward step in the shoe industry.*

Jan Ernst Matzeliger appreciated the opportunities he received in his life, as can be deduced from the fact that he did not merely serve in the shoe making industry but made a lasting dent by inventing a machine that is still in use more than 100 years after his passing. He left his small home country, knowing that if he wanted to do something of lasting magnitude, he had to go where industrialization was in full gear. Upon arriving in the USA, Matzeliger clearly appreciated the opportunity he was given as an immigrant of color in a still heavily segregated world to study the engineering process that led to his proud invention. While he never saw the machine in operation, he died with the awareness that his work would change the way shoes were made, and that was more than many in this industry could say.

*Very few people would think a person could still become hugely successful after failing the national college entrance exam three times, being rejected as a waiter based on physical shortcomings (too small, too skinny, and not good looking), getting turned*

---

[4] https://www.biography.com/inventors/jan-matzeliger
[5] Biography.com (June 24, 2020). *Jan Matzeliger*. Retrieved from https://www.biography.com/inventors/jan-matzeliger

*down from 31 job applications in a row, and being the only one in a group of 24 applicants to not get hired in spite of having earned a college education. This is a snapshot of Jack Ma's preliminary professional story. The man literally struggled to accomplish his vision, and was not even supported by his family, who felt that he was just wasting his time with these ambitious goals.*

*Upon finally being accepted to college, however, Ma made great strides on his educational journey, becoming chairman of the student union and consistently ranking in the top five student performers. He ultimately earned a Bachelor of Arts degree in English, upon which he became a lecturer in English and international trade.*

*When Jack learned about the Internet in the early 1990s, he decided to put his skills in English to use in combination with this new opportunity and started an online Chinese translation agency. An entrepreneur at heart, he remained on high alert about the developments of the day and during his first trip to the US, learned of opportunities that had not yet been explored in China. An example is a website about Chinese beer, which attracted several potential investors within hours after launching. This further sharpened Ma's awareness of the power of the Internet, and he continued to explore opportunities. Even though he did not know how to build websites, he used his educational background, business savvy, and eloquence to impress investors, and hired people who could apply the technical skills he lacked. He started Alibaba around the turn of the millennium and acquired seed capital from US and Japanese financial institutions to establish an e-commerce platform for online Chinese enterprises. Alibaba skyrocketed into one of China's most prominent high-tech holding companies. Meanwhile, Ma founded and sold several other successful ventures as well.*

*While he has now stepped down from the board of Alibaba and pulled out of the public eyes, Ma managed to celebrate the experiences he generated richly. At the time of writing this review, Ma had taken on a position as visiting professor. His net worth still runs in the multiple billions. He has made a profound shift in his focus by supporting social causes, especially in the environmental realm. He has become an advocate for eradicating shark fishing, elevating women's fair treatment and advancement in business, and support small business owners.*

Jack Ma's story is an encouragement to anyone who is ready to give up. His first college entrance exam grades were so atrocious that most others might have accepted that they were not college material. Ma decided to try again and again, and when he finally got admitted, he made sure he exceeded all expectations. This pattern of behaving did not stop there: it seemed that he converted every rejection in one area into victory in another. He cultivated the skills he needed, and put them to work toward a flourishing, unprecedented career. He created light in the darkness by making a difference, to the Chinese business world, and by helping those in need through a variety of philanthropic endeavors.

> **Point to Ponder**
>
> Reflect on your professional life.
> How do you generally appreciate your experiences?
> Please share an example of appreciating a happy and gratifying experience.
> Please share an example of appreciating a dreadful or disappointing experience.

## Appreciating: Being the Light

Inspired by Gandhi's famous statement, "Be the change you want to see in the world", I invite you to become the *light* you want to see around you. You will not be spared the ups and downs of life's roller coaster, but as we have learned from Epictetus and Victor Frankl, you can alter the way you look at your experiences. That is the essence of this chapter: appreciating all the lemons that life throws at you and make lemonade.

This is also a healthy way of living your life: not dwelling on negative thoughts but contemplating the sometimes-hidden light in an apparent darkness. Some losses are hard to digest, and seeing the light or, stronger even—being the light, might sound utopian. Of course you are allowed to be sad when something happens that touches you. Crying, for instance, is a healthy response to the loss of a partner, family member, job, or any other sense of security. But in most cases you will learn to discover a bright side, even if it takes some time.

And if there is no bright side to be seen, there is one thing you should not underestimate: you can become a stronger person through the experience and develop the ability to help others later in dealing with similar situations. There are many people who survived a very traumatic situation, only to become awareness agents –"lights"- to help future groups cope.

Also, some situations, especially change-based, may make you uncomfortable at first, as they feel like bad news. But what sounds like bad news at first may transform into something good once new opportunities emerge. A lot of the time you might not have explored those opportunities if the change had not happened.

Let us now consider how Jan Matzeliger and Jack Ma, our two exemplars in this chapter, dealt with several aspects surrounding their appreciation of what they generated in life:

## Reflection

Based on the short story we shared of Matzeliger, it became clear that he had at least two major reflective instances in his life: when he decided to leave his country to be exposed to greater opportunities, and when he started looking into ways to exchange the manual production of shoes into a mechanized process. In Jack Ma's case, he also reflected multiple times: when he repeatedly failed his college entrance exam, and his family told him he was wasting his time, he decided that he was going to continue studying and trying until he would succeed. Ma reflected on the many opportunities the Internet could offer once he learned about it. He also reflected on ways to get investors on board for his entrepreneurial ideas. All these examples demonstrate how important reflecting is when we want to place any experience in the right and most encouraging perspective.

## Suffering

There is no doubt that both men experienced their share of suffering. Matzeliger was considered a black man in a white world, and experienced discrimination, yet used this negative experience to muster the strength to prove himself. Ma had to stomach an inordinate number of rejections in his early career yet kept working on his skills and kept exploring opportunities until he encountered a breakthrough. Both men used their suffering to become stronger and more determined in accomplishing major goals.

## Perspectives

There is also no doubt that both, Matzeliger and Ma were smart people, just like you who currently reads this. It's important to know what we continuously must work on our self-perspective, but also on the way we decide to look at what is presented to us. Keeping the words of Epictetus and Victor Frankl (cited at the beginning of this chapter) in mind will be a major liberating feat.

## Choice

Both, Matzeliger and Ma, were well aware of the choices they had in life, and based on their reflections, they developed a vision and a path toward accomplishing it. It's important to know that we always have choices, even if the alternatives are not always appealing. The art of living is to make choices that seem good given the insufficient information you have at hand. Know this: you will never have all the information to make a completely informed decision. When your choice seems to lead to less favorable outcomes, you will have to adjust, and thankfully, there will always be some useful tool at hand to do so.

## Change

Even though he lived almost two centuries ago, Matzeliger encountered major changes that required a change of circumstances, and an adjustment of previous intentions. He displayed the flexibility and eagerness to learn, in order to make the changes in his life successful. This was also the case for Jack Ma, who displayed the flexibility to shift his career in multiple directions yet with shrewd use of the skills he had developed. His eloquence in English and entrepreneurial savvy opened many doors to enable him to maneuver through the changes, such as emergence of the Internet, he encountered.

> **Point to Ponder**
>
> Between reflection, suffering, perspectives, choice and change: please rank the aspects you consider points of strength in you?
> Share an example how you implemented the selected strength?
> Now, consider the aspects you need to work on.
> Share an example where you could have used this aspect and did not?

Figure 5.1 above depicts the actions and reactions you will most likely encounter in order to appreciate—thus savor—the effects of generating experiences. As was the case with Fig. 4.1, the different colors of the actions, which should also not be seen as the only important elements in the appreciating process, reflect the intensity of each:

- Reflection is a multidimensional practice. Sometimes you will come to favorable conclusions from the reflection process, and at other times, you may feel concerned after reflecting on what happened. Even though change has been mentioned last in this cycle, it is good to keep in mind that reflection is oftentimes triggered by change.

# 5 Appreciating: Valuing the Experiences

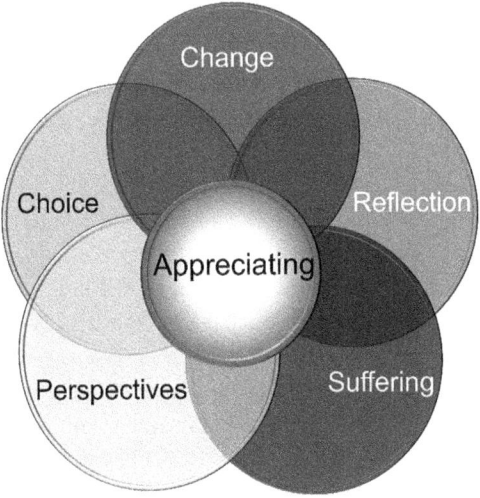

**Fig. 5.1** The process of appreciating

In an article titled, "Don't Underestimate the Power of Self-Reflection," Bailey and Rehman offer the following suggestions to build a habit of reflection.

- *Keep a journal.* This allows you to pause, analyze, and make a note of what happened, how you felt, and what caused you to feel that way. The better you can lay a finger on the how, what, and why of an experience, the easier it becomes to assess everything more deeply later.
- *Take time to review your notes weekly.* Take this practice seriously and don't skip it. Reading your experiences and responses to those experiences later may be somewhat painful or even embarrassing, but at the same time, it is an enlightening practice that will help you understand yourself better.
- *Add to the journal entry when reviewing it.* You may have new insights about the situation that get to the surface when you read. Adding those can complete the picture and provide even more clarity on what happened and why you felt like you did.
- *Contemplate how you can learn* from the reflection and improve where you consider it to be needed. Perhaps you have to tone down your expectations, or adapt better to a situation. Also keep in mind during this process that reflecting can be hard on the ego, but in the end it leads to excellence.[6]

– Suffering is not always a process of agonizing pain, but it still requires dealing with emotions, often related to the outcomes of your reflections. In

---

[6] Bailey, J. R., and Rehman, S. (March 4, 2022). Don't Underestimate the Power of Self-Reflection. Harvard Business Review. Retrieved from https://hbr.org/2022/03/dont-underestimate-the-power-of-self-reflection

Buddhist psychology, suffering is considered one of the foundational Noble Truths, because in life we often suffer, either because we crave something that seems out of our reach, or because we want to release something that we feel stuck with. Suffering is therefore depicted as a dark mental place to be.

In a well-written article, Dr. Tal Ben-Shahar points out that the Western world perceives suffering as something unwelcome: something to be rejected, while the other cultures, especially in the East, suffering is perceived as a useful practice toward greater insight. Citing a prominent Tibetan Buddhist monk, Khenchen Konchog Gyaltshen Rinpoche, Ben-Shahar lists four benefits of suffering:

- *Wisdom:* It is when things are troubling that you reflect and question several aspects of your life. You become more mindful as you contemplate on your experiences and learn to see things in a deeper perspective.
- *Resilience:* As you suffer, you gain strength and become more resilient, so you can endure future hardships with more ease. Imagine the gym, and the pain you feel in your muscles before they get stronger: something similar happens with your emotions.
- *Compassion:* Through your suffering you become aware of the suffering of others and begin to realize that this is a universal emotion that links us all together. You can only become capable of true compassion when you have suffered as well, because then you can place yourself in others' shoes.
- *Deep respect for reality:* suffering is the other side of rejoicing, like yin and yang. You need both experiences to engender a true respect for reality. If your life was filled with only joy and victory, you would not be able to relate to the downside. Through suffering, you become aware of the balance and the ups and downs that make life worthwhile. Suffering infuses humility in you, which is needed to appreciate your accomplishments, especially when they happen after failure.[7]

- Perspectives usually bring some light in sight. Once you have assessed your experience and what it caused, you can start evaluating your options.

It is important to consider how you can broaden your perspectives, and thereby, obtain an expanded view of the world. After all, you're not the only one in the world, and you can rest assured that everyone else has their own perspectives, most likely differing from yours.

- *Expanding your thinking:* If you are willing to open yourself to see and understand the perspectives of others, you might adjust your own perspectives in a

---

[7] Ben-Shahar, T. (2021). The Role of Suffering. *Wholebeing Institute*. Retrieved from https://wholebeinginstitute.com/role-of-suffering/#:~:text=Suffering%20can%20make%20us%20more,pain%20in%20order%20to%20strengthen.

progressive way. When you listen to the perspectives of others, your own thinking gets expanded, as you may hear things you did not consider before.
- *Developing empathy:* when you expose yourself to the perspectives of others and seriously try to understand them, you will start empathizing with their point of view, thus become able to strengthen your relationship with them, and build mutual trust. And as you may already know, trust brings people together and helps them form stronger teams.
- *Increasing inclusion and equity:* by listening and acknowledging others' perspectives, you exude the message of inclusion and equity, and others will feel more appreciated, regardless of any physical, cultural, generational, or other differences there may be.
- *Reducing bias:* Thanks to you opening up to others' perspectives, you become more aware of their driving motives and stances, and may start confronting some of the inbred biases you may have had.
- *Increasing creativity:* What cannot be overlooked is the fact that your exposure to other perspectives will open your mind to other possibilities, and conjure new ideas that you may not have entertained before: a definite win in today's quickly changing world.[8]

- Choice is the furthering of the perspective process: at the choice stage, you engage in strategizing around the options and their potential outcomes, even though you should always keep in mind that choices are made without the full scope at hand, so even when you have made a decision, there may still come a moment that you may have to adjust your path.

Choice is an interesting subject in and of its own. Did you know that the human brain likes choices, but gets demoralized if confronted with too many options? A team of researchers investigated this topic and agreed that there is a definite advantage to choosing. Making our own choice gives us a sense of control and motivates us to strive toward making our selection a success, as opposed to having no option. Yet, several tests have proven that we must be cautious about the number of choices we offer. A limited number of options works more fulfilling than a broad range. Tests have shown that people who may select from a limited number of options (about 5 to 9) are more prone to actually make a choice, compared to those who are offered a very wide range of choices. The explanation is, that when we get confronted with choice overload, it demoralizes our brain. The expansive range becomes cognitively unmanageable, which makes decision-makers feel overwhelmed, confused, less motivated to choose and less satisfied.[9]

---

[8] The Value of Different Perspectives in Professional and Learning Environments (April 21, 2023). *Maryville University*. Retrieved from https://online.maryville.edu/blog/gaining-understanding-different-perspectives/

[9] Scaffifi Abbate, C. and Micelli, S. (July 12, 2022). On the advantages and disadvantages of choice. Preprints.org. Retrieved from https://www.preprints.org/manuscript/202207.0185/v1

- Change is the consolidation of your opining process. Some management gurus have likened the stage of change to a new status quo, as if you are "refreezing" your habits and practices until the next experience triggers this process all over again.

While change, in this chapter, is addressed as the new status quo following a transition process, it might be useful to dwell for a moment on some of the reasons why change (in the concept of transition) is a good thing:

- *It enhances personal growth*: With every change, positive or not, and desired or not, you learn something new. When you learn something new your perspectives expand, and you make mental progress that can benefit you in future situations.
- *It makes you more flexible*: The more you go through changes, the more you will get acquainted with the process, and the easier it will befall you when you have to deal with yet another shift in your life.
- *It brings improvement*: If you keep a positive outlook on change, you will find that every change process can also bring improvement, if not immediately, then definitely in the long run. Remember: everything happens for a good reason, even if you may not see the purpose right away.
- *It can enrich your values*: When a change is major or compelling, it puts you to evaluate your life, and you may find that the insights you obtain from the change have a deepening or positively shifting effect on your values.
- *It makes you stronger*: Confirming the first point above, every change, desired or not, will make you stronger, and enhance your resilience.
- *It may open the path to new opportunities*: Sometimes even the most dreaded change ultimately paves the way to new opportunities that you did not consider before. Due to the changed circumstances in your life, you may find the time or obtain the awareness to embark on new endeavors that can be far more fulfilling than your prior circumstances.
- *It triggers newness*: Very much in line with the focus of this book, change leads to new situations and provides you the opportunity to renew yourself as well.[10]

In Chap. 6, we take pause before stepping into the action from our decision process during the generating stage.

---

[10] Alexander, A. (ND). 10 Powerful Benefits of Change and Why We Should Embrace It. *Tiny Buddha*. Retrieved from https://tinybuddha.com/blog/10-powerful-benefits-of-change-why-embrace-it/

## Chapter Highlights

- *Attitude is everything:* You may not be able to influence everything you experience, but you have the power to decide how to perceive it.
- *Become the light you want to see around you.* You will not be spared the ups and downs of life's roller coaster, but we can alter the way we look at our experiences.
- *Do not dwell on negative thoughts.* Rather, contemplate the sometimes-hidden light in an apparent darkness. If there is no bright side to be seen, you can become a stronger person through the experience and develop the ability to help others later in dealing with similar situations.
- *Aspects surrounding appreciation of what you generated*

  - *Reflection:* this is a multidimensional emotion. Sometimes you will come to favorable conclusions from the reflection process, and at other times, you may feel depressed or concerned after reflecting on what happened.
  - *Suffering:* This often related to the outcomes of your reflections. In life we often suffer, either because we crave something that seems out of our reach, or because we want to release something that we feel stuck with.
  - *Perspectives:* Once you have assessed your experience and what it caused, you can start evaluating your options.
  - *Choice:* This is where you engage in strategizing around the options and their potential outcomes.
  - *Change:* This is the consolidation of your opining process. Some management gurus have likened the stage of change to a new status quo, as if you are "refreezing" your habits and practices until the next experience triggers this process all over again.

# 6

# Internalizing: Bringing It All into Scope

**Contents**
Spiritual Beings.................................................................................................. 69
Internalizing: The Path Toward Responsible Newness...................................... 75
Chapter Highlights............................................................................................ 81

**Abstract** This chapter is more philosophical in nature, explaining the importance to regularly reflect on the things you went through, and internalize the message you extract from them. It links back to Chap. 2, where insight meditation was discussed. It invites you to consider several ways to enhance your insight in the entire scope of your life and points to Chap. 8 for more detail therein. Regular reflections on your experiences (generation) and the way you decide to look at them and store them in your psyche (appreciation) will be of great importance toward the way you decide to internalize the progress of your life. The importance of contemplation, mindfulness, paradigm shifts, resilience, and gratitude will be discussed in this chapter.

**The Awakening: A Story**
A very popular celebrity who had traveled the world round and seen a lot of beautiful places during his performances, had acquired a lingering attitude of dissatisfaction that he just couldn't get rid of. He could not be charmed by the beauty and kindness of the people around him, did not enjoy the delicious food that was prepared for him, and did not care of the exquisite cars he had in his humongous garage.

One day, the celebrity got into his private jet and took off, even though the tower at the local airport had advised against it. Soon he realized why: dark clouds surrounded his small jet and he got disoriented. Even though he was an experienced pilot, he could not make sense of what was going on and decided to ascend some more. By now he had lost contact with the tower and couldn't trust his dashboard.

Somehow, our friend managed to land somewhere, even though he couldn't recall later how that happened. Once safely on the ground, he stayed motionless in his seat for quite some time, but then got out and was surprised to find that he couldn't figure out where he was.

The celebrity got back in his seat and closed his eyes. He wasn't sure if he had been sleeping or simply drifted away in a deep meditation, but when he came through he realized how many reasons for gratitude there were in his life so far. He also became aware that he took all his blessings for granted and had been a true jerk to many people.

The next time the celebrity opened his eyes he saw an old women hovering over him. She said, "Your mission here is completed. You have awakened and are advised never to forget how blessed you have been and still are!"

The old women disappeared, and the next thing our friend remembered was that he landed safely at the small private airport from where he had initially taken off.

Once back in his familiar environment, the celebrity was a changed person. Everyone wondered what happened to bring about this major change in him, but all he said to everyone was: "internalizing, my friend, internalizing…".

---

> We have to understand there are two parts of our mind, there's the conscious and the subconscious. It's the subconscious that controls our behavior. It's the conscious mind where the intellect is resident. So the conscious mind is understanding information, but it's not internalizing it.[1]
>
> ~ *Bob Proctor*

**Grateful**

Turn inward and enjoy the light
Of nirvana
Inhale at the tune of a sacred inner song
So serene, so beautiful
It makes you want to cry

---

[1] https://www.azquotes.com/quote/1162731?ref=internalizing

Peek in the dark corners of your soul
Face your silent fears
And be grateful for their existence
As they keep you grounded
And remind you of the ingeniously
Disguised layer of sensitivity
That keeps your eyes open
And your empathy alive


Be grateful for all that you are
For the path that led you here
And the one that will lead you onward
Be grateful for the blessings
And for the setbacks that made you stronger
There's nothing wrong with a little self-reflection
And a healthy sense of humble gratitude
For being you

*–Joan Marques*

## Spiritual Beings

We are spiritual beings going through a human experience. This is a mindset that several scholars and practitioners in the management world share. In the Academy of Management, this group of scholars and practitioners are even connected in a division, the Management, Spirituality and Religion Division, in which yours truly has served on the leadership track from 2021 through 2026. It is refreshing to communicate about the insight of being primarily spiritual beings with such an eclectic, globally dispersed group of thinkers and doers.

When you think about being a spiritual being having a human experience, your perspective widens, and the human element becomes a by-product of a more essential whole. You transcend the limitation of only caring for one species in such a rich mosaic of living entities. You also obtain a renewed respect for all that lives, realizing that this may not necessarily be the only experience we will have in the cycle(s) of life.

Yet, whether you believe in recurring life cycles or not, respect for all beings is good. It underscores Thich Nhat Han's earlier discussed concept of interbeing. We inter-are. In order for us to live in this world, we are dependent on so many other beings, not just humans. Just consider the many products we use that are given to us by animals: milk, butter, honey, meat and fish (if you are a meat or fish eater), and the fact that so many of our non-human fellow inhabitants of this earth fertilize our plants in order for them to bear fruit and present us with a breathtakingly beautiful nature.

One thing that we, especially in the Western part of the world, have become alienated to, is the fact that, as spiritual beings, we are capable of finding the answers to everything within. For those of us who practice vipassana (insight) meditation, this awareness goes even further: we can allow our mind to reconnect with its ability to practice Mettā, through which we can help ourselves and others. Mettā requires a selfless approach, void of selfishness, and driven by loving-kindness. The Vipassana Research Institute (VRI) recommends practicing Mettā through vipassana meditation, as this will establish the proper mindset. This proper mindset entails the understanding that true happiness is not tied to obtaining or releasing any practice, position or possession, but is void of such cravings and aversions. When there is a genuine mindset of every being to be happy, we can practice Mettā.[2]

> *In 2008, I participated in a 10-day Vipassana retreat in McLeod Ganj, a suburb of Dharamshala, Himachal Pradesh, India. As many people who have gone through this experience will tell you, it can be challenging, especially in the first few days, to sit for so many hours in a row and meditate. The first four days, especially, can feel tedious, due to the sole focus on your breath. But the overall experience is a priceless asset, as it helps the practitioner generate so many insights that were dormant and unexplored.*
>
> *During the retreat, there is no conversation between anyone. Everything happens in silence. You also pledge to refrain from unwholesome acts, among which killing, which means that flies, spiders, or any other living thing should be respected in its existence.*
>
> *The four initial days of breathing focus clearly fulfill an important purpose: they silence the mind, and make the practitioners aware of the power of our breath. Then, when the scanning of the entire body starts, a fascinating awareness arises about being your body as a vehicle – a temple – in which the spirit resides. These examinations or scans make you well aware of areas in your body that need some more attention.*

---

[2] Vipassana Research Institute (August, 2008). *The Practice of Mettā-Bhāvanā*. Retrieved from https://www.vridhamma.org/node/2377#:~:text=The%20practice%20of%20mett%C4%81-bh%C4%81van%C4%81%20%28meditation%20of%20loving%20kindness%29,calming%2C%20positive%20vibrations%20of%20pure%20and%20compassionate%20love

*Then, when the practice of Mettā is presented, you learn how you can focus on those areas that may need healing, and you send positive energy to them. While I cannot speak for others, I have found in the many years since this precious experience, that practicing Mettā has been a true blessing to me.*

*As I was writing one of the previous chapters, I felt one of my old ailments, gastritis, emerging. Whenever I encounter stressful situations – and I am currently experiencing a very stressful episode at my work – my stomach starts acting up. Fortunately, I remembered Mettā, and focused on the spot where the dull ache deep inside was bothering me and causing unpleasant sequences of belching. I was happy to find that the next morning, things were a lot better, and the belching that I had been troubled by two days before, was strongly reduced. Engaging in some self-exploration as I write this, I realize that I should repeat the exercise, which I intend to do before going to sleep.*

*This short admission is not intended to tell anyone that they should stop going to the doctor or stop taking medication. That would be downright irresponsible and troublesome. But we should not underestimate the power we have, as spiritual beings – to invest positive energy into our bodies, and maybe even into the bodies of those we care for.*

In returning to GAIN, and the process of Internalizing, there is another aspect to consider. Internalizing results in a heightened level of consciousness that you would not entertain if you were to scurry through your daily life without taking the time to silently turn inward. Internalizing is like reflecting, but then with capital letters. Sometimes you may have to engage in a broader scope of contemplation, because some things may have a recurring nature, which may indicate that there are deeper reasons at their foundation. Remember the teachers I mentioned earlier? Some teachers just don't leave, because you did not internalize the lesson they were sent to teach you. Teachers, which are mainly situations from which you should learn something, will only disappear when you have internalized the lesson.

Internalizing does not mean that you should dwell in the past, however. Contemplating on past experiences in this instance is only good if you need to detect a pattern, so that you can address it at its roots, and be able to move on from the situation after the internalization process.

Also, internalizing can be done in multiple ways. If you are not a meditator, you can internalize through simple sitting on your front or back porch and think things through. Or you can write about the situation. Keeping a journal can be very enlightening, as it will provide you a written overview of things that happened before and can reveal patterns you may not have discovered before. Long walks in silent are also very therapeutic. Try to choose a calm and inspirational environment for your thoughtful stroll, and you may find answers you have not considered before.

> **Point to Ponder**
>
> Reflect on your daily practices.
> Are you finding the time to internalize your practices, decisions, and perspectives?
> If so, when do you do that?
> If not, how could you build this valuable practice into your day from now on?

The purpose of this chapter, as stated in the introduction, is to encourage you to take some time through your day to contemplate on the things that trouble you, and preferably also on the general path of your life.

> *General Colin Powell, born in New York City out of Jamaican parents, has been my role model for many years. General Powell was the first African American chairman of the Joint Chiefs of Staff in the U.S. Army, and a force onto himself. When I decided to immigrate to the US, I bought the first edition of his now famous book, "My American Journey", and found much encouragement in his reflections. Powell was not a brilliant kid by any stretch. In fact, he described himself as normal and even mediocre in school performance When he attended City College of New York he entered military service, which he did for the next 35 years, serving in Vietnam, West Germany and South Korea, while also acting as President Ronald Reagan's Deputy National Security Advisor in 1987. In 1989 he became National Security Advisor and was promoted the next year to the rank of general. Under President George H.W. Bush he made it to Chairman of the Joint Chiefs of Staff, overseeing almost 30 crises, among which Operation Desert Storm in 1991. He retired in 1993, and devoted his attention to a social cause by founding America's Promise, an organization helping at-risk children. Then, in 2000, he became George W. Bush's Secretary of State.*
>
> *His term started out with a focus on diplomatic alliances throughout the world and supporting peace in the Middle East. As the terrorist attacks of September 11 2001 hit the nation, Powell's term became dominated by the challenges the Bush Administration faced. When the attention shifted to Iraq, Powell presented intelligence to the UN that supported the claim that Iraq had weapons of mass destruction and could produce more. In hindsight, parts of the intelligence were found to be erroneous. The crises continued with issues in Afghanistan, Russia, and China, and Powell focusing on improving relationships. Near the end of 2004, Powell announced his resignation, after which he re-devoted his time on America's Promise Alliance, while also serving the Boards of Directors of the Council on Foreign Relations, the Eisenhower Fellowship Program, and the Powell Center at the City College of New York.*[3]

---

[3] *Biographies of the Secretaries of State: Colin Luther Powell* (1937–2021). Department of State—Office of the Historian. Retrieved from https://history.state.gov/departmenthistory/people/powell-colin-luther

## 6 Internalizing: Bringing It All into Scope

*In retirement, Powell continued to be a vocal source on political topics, openly criticizing the Bush administration on a number of issues. In September 2006, Powell joined moderate Senate Republicans in supporting more rights and better treatment for detainees at the Guantanamo detention facility. In October 2008, he made headlines again with his endorsement of Barack Obama for president.[4]*

*Mr. Powell's character was significantly strengthened through his self-reflections and his experiences, and he became a great motivator to others. I love his statement, "Perpetual optimism is a force multiplier.[5]" He explains this as follows, "I am talking about a gung-ho attitude that says 'we can change things here, we can achieve awesome goals, we can be the best. 'Spare me the grim litany of the 'realist;' give me the unrealistic aspirations of the optimist any day."*

*Powell deserves to be described as a resilient individual, having undoubtedly experienced racism throughout his life and career and learning to grow stronger in the face of adversity. He must have internalized frequently and strongly on his experiences and the way he could interpret them, and the fact that in the last few decades of his life he diligently kept serving as a member of a political party that let him down and of which he had serious concerns shows more character than many of us can understand.*

Colin Powell wrote two books about his life, which reveals that he must have done some deep thinking about his human journey. There were many honorable moments, but there were also painful ones, which he had to overcome, right when he thought that he would be able to retire peacefully. The greatness of this man can be detected in the fact that, in spite of having been set up for failure, he remained loyal to those he had pledged his support to. Not everyone appreciates this. Some people feel that staying where you are no longer appreciated is like committing moral suicide. I believe Powell had too much backbone to check out. He was vocal in his disappointment, became an endorser for members of other political teams, but did not formally abandoned his troops.

*Vandana Shiva is a courageous Indian scholar and environmental activist who is particularly known for her participation in the anti-GMO movement. GMO stands for Genetically Modified Organisms. She was born in a family where love for nature's wellness was a high priority. Her father was a conservator of forests, and her mother was a farmer who loved nature. To underscore why Shiva knows what she is talking about: she is a physicist, ecologist, activist, editor, and author of numerous books. She founded Navdanya, a movement for biodiversity conservation and farmers' rights. Navdanya means "Nine Seeds" or "New Gift". The organization, an NGO, is very*

---

[4] Biography: Famous Political Figures-Black History. Colin Powell. Retrieved from https://www.biography.com/political-figures/colin-powell

[5] https://www.azquotes.com/quote/578076

outspoken in areas of protecting the diversity and integrity of living resources, especially native seed, the promotion of organic farming and fair trade.[6] In addition, Dr. Shiva founded and manages the Research Foundation for Science, Technology and Natural Resource Policy. Her purpose is to advocate changes in the way agriculture and food are monopolized by a small group of giant companies. Dr. Shiva is a constructive globetrotter, having assisted grassroots organizations of the Green movement in Africa, Asia, Latin America, Ireland, Switzerland, and Austria with campaigns against genetic engineering.[7]

Vandana Shiva courageously supports the idea of seed freedom, or the rejection of patents on new plant lines or cultivars. She campaigns against patenting life forms, calling the patenting of life 'biopiracy'. Her campaigns have successfully targeted the efforts of major corporations who were trying to patent indigenous plants, such as basmati. On the other hand she opposed genetically modified rice, calling it more harmful than beneficial. Her efforts are oftentimes criticized, such as in 2013, when two economists calculated that the absence of Golden Rice in India had caused the loss of over 1.4 million life man years in the previous ten years.[8] However, Shiva has her own strong theories on the destructive effects of GMOs, claiming that excessive high seed prices from monopolistic corporate giants lead to surging farmers' debts and consequential suicide.

When reading through the arguments on either side, there is primarily moral and sustainability-based sense in Shiva's perspectives, and economic sense in her opponents' viewpoints. Critics of Shiva also reveal her expensive demands to conduct lectures, thereby pointing out that she herself if not making any financial sacrifices. Her former husband, a scientist, has also written several articles debunking Shiva's claims.

Vandana Shiva is a controversial figure, with seemingly as many supporters as opponents. Her fight against genetically modifying food is a moral one, and she has been able to voice her stance on several global forums. The monopolization of seeds, as has been infamously spearheaded by global giants such as Monsanto, is also a serious aspect that demands greater awareness. Shiva collaborates with other environmental scientists in promoting inner shifts in perspectives to help us respond more skillfully to climate and environmental crises. In these collaborative meetings, the scientists call for connecting internally and become aware of our interconnectedness with the natural world. They promote contemplative practices such as mindfulness and meditation was effective ways to deepen our sense of oneness with the living universe around us.[9]

---

[6] "*Navdanya Indian agricultural project*". Encyclopædia Britannica. Retrieved Dec. 31, 2023.

[7] *Vandana Shiva*. Humans Nature. Retrieved from https://humansandnature.org/vandana-shiva/

[8] Wesseler, J.; Zilberman, D. (2014). "The economic power of the Golden Rice opposition". Environment and Development Economics. 19 (1): 1.

[9] "Can inner shifts in perspectives help us respond more skillfully to the climate and environmental crisis?" https://sciwizlive.com/event/deep-ecology-mindfulness-climate-emergency-insights-from-scientists-and-contemplative-traditions/

# Internalizing: The Path Toward Responsible Newness

Practicing internalization will always be a good thing. Taking some time at the end of every day to conduct a moral scan on what all has transpired, how you reacted and what went through your mind is a great way to practice mindfulness. The intention is, that spending 30 minutes at the end of a day may gradually lead to multiple short reflective moments through the day.

Let us now analyze how we might interpret Colin Powell's and Vandana Shiva's behaviors related to internalization.

## Contemplation

Having held high profile positions with immense responsibilities, it should easily be deduced that both, Powell and Shiva must have done a lot of contemplating on their actions, their strategies, and the way they were perceived. Both of these people have endured being ostracized at some points in their career, which usually augments a persons' self-examination, and enforces turning inward.

## Mindfulness

Powell's aptitude for a mindful approach can be detected from what he mainly focused on in his position as international representative of the US. He was an advocate of negotiating in a respectful way with all parties around the table. "I've found, in negotiations, always get yourself partially on the side of the other person, understand what they need. Always show respect. Even if we're the United States of America, I've always tried to show respect to the smallest country in the world that wants us to do something with them. No country is unimportant. No person is unimportant."[10]

Shiva's entire mission as an environmental activist is founded on mindfulness. While global giants make some powerful statements about the economic advantages of GMOs, she continues to warn about the effects on poor farmers and, most importantly, on our collective health.

---

[10] *Powell's legacy, in admirers' words and his own*. The Harvard Gazette. Retrieved from https://news.harvard.edu/gazette/story/2021/10/colin-powells-legacy-in-admirers-words-and-his-own/

## Paradigm Shifts

As part of their journey, both Powell and Shiva dealt with and called for paradigm shifts. In Powell's acclaimed article, "13 Rules of Leadership[11]", he refers to at least x leadership instances of a paradigm shift: Rule 1, It Ain't as Bad as You Think! It Will Look Better in the Morning; Rule 2, Get Mad Then Get Over It, and Rule 4. It Can be Done. Leaders make things happen. If one approach doesn't work, find another. Each of these three rules point at internalizing, reconsidering, and shifting paradigms when or where needed.

Vandana Shiva calls for a paradigm shift on a regular basis. She targets the unaware masses that support the trends of affluent governments and corporations to monopolize the food supply, and sees fluctuating levels of success while doing so.

## Resilience

Having read about these two people, it's easy to conclude that both Colin Powell and Vandana Shiva are very resilient people. They have both travelled around the world to advocate their purposes, presented before governments and peoples, and found the strength to re-emerge every time they were criticized or their stances debunked. They went ahead and reinvented themselves and their purposes, founded non-governmental organizations serving social causes, and maintained a moral perspective in their initiatives.

## Gratitude

While gratitude is not always visible, there are great instances where both, Colin Powell and Vandana Shiva, demonstrated how grateful they are. In a 2017 article, Kathy Holoman wrote the following:

> *General Powell has been around for EIGHT decades, and he still remembers to thank people for what they do to make his life easier. He thanks all kinds of people – from all walks of life. He muses about the White House janitors who worked hard day-in-and-day-out. He remembers specific soldiers' contributions during his tours-of-duty. He openly expresses gratitude to his wife, Alma. He even takes the time to sincerely thank the people like me who would give their eye teeth to listen to him any time on his national speaker circuit.[12]*

---

[11] Colin Powell's 13 rules of leadership. Retrieved from https://executiveexcellence.com/13-rules-leadership-colin-powell/

[12] Langston Holoman, K. (August 2, 2017). On General Colin Powell, Horse Sense, Gratitude and Growing Two Heads. Linked-In article. Retrieved from https://www.linkedin.com/pulse/general-colin-powell-horse-sense-gratitude-growing-twoholoman/

Vandana Shiva does not let an opportunity go by to express her gratitude and encourage others to remain alert of their own. In her book, Oneness vs The 1%: Shattering Illusions, Seeding Freedom, she wrote:

> *Being a planetary citizen does not need space travel. It means being conscious that we are part of the universe and of the earth. The most fundamental law is to recognize that we share the planet with other beings, and that we have a duty to care for our common home.*[13]

This statement calls for a universal sense of gratitude for our place in the universe, and our role to support one another.

> **Point to Ponder**
>
> Between contemplation, mindfulness, paradigm shifts, resilience, and gratitude: please rank the quality or behavior you consider most strongly represented in you?
> Share an example how you were able to apply the selected strength?
> Now, consider the quality or behavior you need to work on.
> Share an example where you could have used this skill and did not?

Figure 6.1 above shows the actions and behaviors you will most likely come across when you internalize your experiences. The different colors of the elements, which should, again, not be seen as the only important elements in the internalizing process, reflect the intensity of each. In Fig. 6.1, I chose to grant contemplation the darker color, as it is the most intense process in the cycle. The other four behaviors are not necessarily easier, but they can become recurring traits and therefore easier to apply if you keep them intact.

– Contemplation is the very foundation of the internalizing process. It requires a deep dive into your psyche to evaluate, compare and contrast, and intensely cogitate your practices, in order to learn from them, understand them, and, if needed, pave new behavioral pathways in the future.

   There are many advantages to regular contemplation, and here are some good ones:

   - *You learn about yourself:* Even if you are extremely busy, you owe it to yourself to take a few minutes every day to reflect on your day, the things that happened, the choices you made, how you reacted, and how you

---
[13] Shiva, V. (2020). *Oneness vs The 1%: Shattering Illusions, Seeding Freedom.* Chelsea Green Publishing, Chelsea, VT.

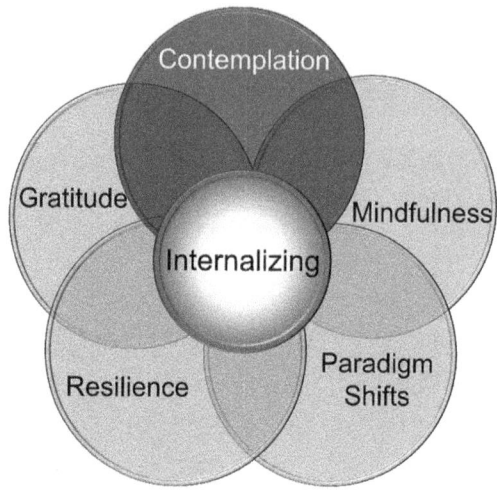

**Fig. 6.1** Internalizing

felt. Thos daily process will help you get to know and understand yourself better, identify your strengths and weaknesses, thus enable you to cultivate the strengths and address the weaknesses.

- *You learn from your past*: If you contemplate on the longer scope of your life, you will discover some recurring patterns from which you could learn. The changes you can decide to make could make your life and your choices so much more rewarding.
- *Your actions are more thoughtful*: Contemplation takes away some of the ad-hoc approaches so many of us have toward the things we need to do. If you contemplate first, you will most likely make more moderate decisions, and will be able to become more closely aligned with your true goals, maintain better connections, and find greater peace and joy in your life.[14]

– Mindfulness is a practice that comes forth from turning inward and contemplating a situation. Mindfulness intensifies as you contemplate more. It can become a valuable skill in your life.

Thich Nhat Hanh, the revered Vietnamese Zen master who passed away in 2022, made many statements to underscore the importance of mindfulness in

---

[14] Gordon-Mead, W. (June 2, 2021). The Power of Contemplation: 10 Ways to Harness Greater Peace and Joy. *Thrive Global*. Retrieved from https://community.thriveglobal.com/the-power-of-contemplation-10-ways-to-harness-greater-peace-and-joy/

our life. He asserted, among others that mindfulness keeps us present in the moment. By being mindful, we can better understand ourselves and our suffering, and practice compassion toward ourself. It is, after all, important to love yourself, so that you can love others as well.

Thich thereby brings in the concept of interbeing, which is discussed in this book in multiple locations. Interbeing is a profound concept that helps us understand how connected we are to all beings: human and non-human. Interbeing makes us aware that we live interdependently with everyone and everything around us. Interbeing is simply a more easily comprehensible term for dependent co-arising, which is a foundational concept in Buddhist teaching. Interbeing—or dependent co-arising—wakes us up from the notion of being separated from others.

When we practice mindfulness, we learn to keep ourselves calm and peaceful, and do away with the anxiety that society can place on us so easily. Thanks to mindfulness we can awaken to what really matters, and maybe help others to become mindful as well.[15]

– Paradigm Shifts, in the personal realm, are perspective changes that can occur through multiple ways of obtaining new insights. One of those is when you engage in deep contemplation, and learn to perceive things differently. While others can nudge you in a certain direction, you are the only one who can apply a paradigm shift for yourself.

A paradigm shift is considered a major change in worldview, concepts, and practices, whereby a previous paradigm gets replaced by the new one. This can pertain to the process itself, or the implementation of a process. In the industry realm, paradigm shifts happen with new inventions that radically change the way things were done.

We are used to maintaining paradigms, as they are our interpretation of reality. Paradigms may not be perfect, but they are helpful for making sense of otherwise complex processes. As you can imagine, we have undergone far more paradigm shifts in the last hundred years than in multiple centuries together! The internet is one of the major paradigm shifters in our lifetime.

For business organizations it is important to be aware of new paradigms, as refraining from doing so could mean becoming obsolete and meaningless.

As interpreted in this book, you can also experience a paradigm shift if your worldview fundamentally changes to a new state from a previous one. If, for

---

[15] Shukhman, H. (Nov. 16, 2022). Message from Henry: Mindful Presence. *Mountain Cloud Zen Center*. Retrieved from https://www.mountaincloud.org/message-from-henry-mindful-presence/?gad_source=1-&gclid=Cj0KCQiAhomtBhDgARIsABcaYymRLjdhwfWIz8WUvq1DiE0QJmWldjoDNOMY12gkW zHKA4SMWswEMeQaAlNQEALw_wcB

instance, you convert to a new religion, move to a new country that is vastly different in its development than the one where you came from, or internalize the impressions in your life using deep contemplation, you can experience a paradigm shift, particularly is your new way of thinking replaces the old one.[16]

– Resilience can be tough to apply based on the severity of a situation, but it is a long-term skill that makes you stronger and can become an immensely strong trait in dealing with adversities and having to reinvent yourself.

Life presents enough challenges to understand that resilience is a critical characteristic for us to develop and maintain. In each of the areas of our life, work, home, or society, there are numerous adversities that can happen and that will require for us to bounce back.

Resilience is an expression of strength, but it doesn't mean that the situation leaves you free from stress or trauma. After each challenging encounter, you will still have to recuperate, but you will also become stronger through the resilience you practice.

There are ample advantages to being resilient. If you can bounce back, you have demonstrated strength, and that will be appreciated by your surroundings, and not least of all by you! And because we experience more challenges in today's world than before, we develop more flexibility and courage, every time we have to tap into our resilience.

Resilient employees in a work environment can keep the team together and demonstrate leadership in keeping things running while others need to be supported and encouraged to continue performing.

Resilient people also demonstrate greater emotional stability and possibly even better physical and mental health, as they manage to keep themselves level-headed in the fact of adversity.[17]

– Gratitude is also a valuable feeling that we often don't consider in our daily practices. Yet, there is so much to be grateful for, and it feels good—to yourself and others—if you regularly express how thankful you are for the blessings you encounter.

---

[16] Hayes, A. (Dec. 1, 2022). What Is a Paradigm Shift? Definition, Example, and Meaning. *Investopedia*. Retrieved from https://www.investopedia.com/terms/p/paradigm-shift.asp

[17] Duszynski-Goodman, l. (Oct 17, 2023) What Is Resilience? How to Build Resiliency, Benefits and More. *Forbes*. https://www.forbes.com/health/mind/resilience/

A Harvard health publication suggested, among other things, the following useful ways to cultivate gratitude:

- *Write thank-you notes.* The make the received and the sender (you) happier. If you make sending thank-you notes a habit, you will reap the rewards through a more solid circle of devoted and positively minded connections.
- *Send thoughts of gratitude:* Don't underestimate the power of the mind. If you cannot find the time, send your gratitude mentally.
- *Keep a gratitude* journal: If you can make it a habit to write down a few reasons why you are grateful on a daily basis, you will find that your innate sense of being grateful will grow.
- *Count your blessings*: Sit at least once a week with a pencil and paper and write down all the blessings you experienced. You'll be amazed what comes rolling out if you make this a habit.
- Pray and/or meditate: If you are religious you can pray to express your gratitude. You can also meditate. This can be done as an alternative to praying or in addition to. Mindfulness meditation helps you to focus on the here and now with a non-judging mind.[18]

## Chapter Highlights

- *We are spiritual beings going through a human experience.* Thinking this way helps your perspective to widen, with the human element becoming a by-product of a more essential whole.
- *Respect for all beings is good.* It underscores Thich Nhat Han's concept of interbeing. In order for us to live in this world, we are dependent on so many other beings, not just humans.
- *Internalizing results in a heightened level of consciousness* that you would not entertain if you were to scurry through your daily life without taking the time to silently turn inward.
- *Internalizing can be done in multiple ways*: through meditation, silent contemplation, keeping a journal taking a long walk are all effective options.
- *Practicing internalization will always be a good thing.* Taking some time at the end of every day to conduct a moral scan on what all has transpired, how you reacted and what went through your mind is a great way to practice mindfulness.

---

[18] *Giving thanks can make you happier* (August 14, 2021). Harvard Health Publishing—Harvard Medical School Retrieved from https://www.health.harvard.edu/healthbeat/giving-thanks-can-make-you-happier#:~:text=In%20positive%20psychology%20research%2C%20gratitude,express%20gratitude%20in%20multiple%20ways

– *Useful practices related to internalization:*

- *Contemplation:* This is the foundation of the internalizing process. It requires a deep dive into your psyche to evaluate, compare and contrast, and intensely overthink your practices, in order to learn from them, understand them, and, if needed, pave new behavioral pathways in the future.
- *Mindfulness* comes forth from turning inward and contemplating a situation. Mindfulness intensifies as you contemplate more, and can become a valuable skill in your life.
- *Paradigm Shifts* occur when you engage in deep contemplation, and learn to perceive things differently. While others can nudge you in a certain direction, you are the only one who can apply a paradigm shift for yourself.
- *Resilience* is a long-term skill that makes you stronger and can become an immensely strong trait in dealing with adversities and having to reinvent yourself.
- *Gratitude* is often overlooked in our daily practices. Yet, there is so much to be grateful for, and it feels good to regularly express how thankful you are for the blessings you encounter.

# 7

# Newness: Rebirth Through Enrichment

**Contents**
Understanding Newness........................................................................................... 84
Newness: The Path Toward Continuous Improvement......................................... 89
Chapter Highlights................................................................................................... 96

**Abstract** This chapter marks the final aspect in the GAIN cycle, and at the same time presents the beginning of the next stage of your life. It reminds you that rebirth can be a continuous process of renewing yourself and growing from your experiences. It will also emphasize the challenge of choice in that it is in your own hands (or mind) to decide how you will perceive and proceed on your life's path: as a sequence of defeats and losses, or a sequence of victories and gains. The chapter emphasizes concepts such as self-renewal, innerchange, optimism, open-mindedness, and meaning, among others.

**Liberating Yourself: A Story**
There was a girl named Madhavi, who lived in Gamru Village, in the Northern part of India. Madhavi came from a very poor home, and walked long distances every day to first bring the family's two cows to the pasture before going to school, and picking them up again on the way home. At school, Madhavi kept to herself, as most of the other girls seemed to distance themselves from her.

One of the daily activities in Madhavi's school was a meditation exercise, and she enjoyed the silence during that practice immensely. She particularly liked the idea of releasing old concerns and shifting into newness. To her, this awareness was like a beacon of light in her existence, and it encouraged Madhavi to strive to be her best in everything she did, while not dwelling on any past mishaps.

One day, a group of wealthy business people visited the school, and asked the teachers to recommend their exceptional students. Much to her surprise, Madhavi was called into the principal's office, and learned that, based on her performance, she was eligible for a full-paid scholarship for higher education in the UK!

Madhavi's parents were ecstatic when they heard the news, even though it meant some extra work for the ones who stayed behind.

After several years Madhavi, now a well-educated young woman, returned to Gamru Village and founded an organization that would replicate the good work she had benefited from as a young girl.

One thing she made a mandatory practice for all students who wanted an opportunity to obtain higher education: understanding newness through meditation. Madhavi has since sent many youngsters from poor homes—like hers—for further education and betterment in life.

> There is only one corner of the universe you can be certain of improving, and that's your own self.[1]
>
> ~Aldous Huxley

## Understanding Newness

This is something you may not think of regularly, but from day to day, and even throughout the day, you experience multiple moments of renewal. Every experience you go through, everything you witness or learn, infuses new insights in you, and enhances your perspectives. Once you grasp that, you may also realize then that through these insights, you change. A changed version of you is a new you. It's a spontaneous and continuous process, so we don't dwell on it much, but now and then it's good to remember this.

---

[1] https://www.brainyquote.com/authors/aldous-huxley-quotes

Why is it good? For several reasons. For example: if you did something today that you are not too proud of, and you think it over in the evening, you become aware how to improve the next time. If tomorrow something similar happens, you now apply a different reaction, because you have decided to change your approach. That's your newness in action.

This doesn't just help in your responses to others, but also in your self-perspective. You can forgive yourself because you are no longer the person you were yesterday. Thanks to internalizing yesterday's lesson, you have become a new person.

While this psychological perspective makes sense, there is also a physical way in which you experience newness. That is through apoptosis. Apoptosis is the death of cells, which occurs as a normal and controlled part of an organism's growth or development. In our body, one million cells die every second. About 330 billion of those cells are replaced every day—that's about 1 percent of all our body's cells. So, over the course of seven to ten years, our body has completed a full cycle of cell renewal. That implies that in seven to 10 years you are practically a completely new person, as almost all of your old cells have been replaced. While there may still be a resemblance of the person you were almost a decade ago, you can truly say that you are now a different person.

So, now there are two ways in which you experience renewal: one is through new insights that trigger different behavior, and the other is through a biological process that happens to all living beings.

The greatest insight from all of this may be that life offers each of us so many changes to improve and grow, thanks to our ability to internalize, and then change. These instances of repeated renewal can be defined as our continuous rebirths. And because we have the ability to think things over and adjust our behavior based on that, we can renew ourselves whenever we want to.

People sometimes think that renewal is a religious process, and that it has to do with some born-again movement, or that it depends on a religious philosophy. Nothing wrong with those, and if you have experienced something like that, it's a win. But you don't have to be religious in any way to experience newness, as you have now read. The way we interpret newness in this book is a mental process of adjusting toward progress. That's a profound way of continuous advancement in directions you may not even have considered possible before.

Let's now look at the other side of reality for a frightening moment: staying as you are, without allowing newness in your life. I ran into an article based on a presentation John Gardner delivered to McKinsey & Company in 1990.[2] Gardner wrote a book on self-renewal in 1964, and its contents still make all the sense in the world. In the article I read, Gardner admonished his audience to refrain from living as barnacles. He cited the following findings about their behavior: "The barnacle [...] is confronted with an existential decision about where it's going to live. Once it decides... it spends the rest of its life with its head cemented to a rock[3]". To me, that's a pretty scary description, and I did some reading on barnacles myself after reading this, leading me to wholeheartedly agree that this should not be the way any of us should live our lives.

*Since Gardner's article was so inspiring, I would like to paraphrase some wisdom gems from it and encourage you to read it in its entirety by following the link provided.*

- *Life can be hard and bog you down. Not everyone has the resilience to get up after every defeat or disappointment. And sometimes things can be so demanding that you stop learning and simply start going through the motions or get trapped in fixed patterns and habits.*
- *Life provides more opportunities for renewal than you can foresee, so giving up is really a great disservice to yourself. Circumstances, and sometimes our own attitude, can build mental prisons to which we stand guard without realizing it, we should break through the demoralizing mindsets that curtail our will to seek newness.*
- *There is no age limit to obtaining newness. Some people renew their life patterns even when they approach 80! Learning is something we should never cease to do, and you cannot learn everything from others. Some lessons you will have to learn from experience.*
- *Failing is a natural part of life and an opportunity for growth. Just try to avoid collaborating in your own failures.*
- *There is no perpetual haven. Everything changes. So, keep tapping into your inexhaustible energy and the many gifts you have not yet explored. Get to know yourself, and redefine who you are.*

> **Point to Ponder**
>
> Reflect on an opportunity for renewal you had.
> What was the opportunity?
> Did you seize the opportunity?
> If so, how? If not, what would you have done differently if given the opportunity today?

---

[2] Gardner, J. (November 10, 1990). *Personal Renewal by John Gardner.* Delivered to McKinsey & Company, Phoenix, AZ. Retrieved from https://fs.blog/great-talks/personal-renewal-john-gardner/
[3] Ibid, par. 4.

## 7   Newness: Rebirth Through Enrichment

Experiencing newness is nothing new. It's just that not everyone refers to it as such. Some people make a deliberate choice to reinvent themselves from a previous lifestyle, while others undergo a sequence of situations that instigate a paradigm shift leading to newness. Regardless of the nature in which this happens, newness is a stage that usually reveals improvement in a person's demeanor and lifestyle.

> *Robert Downey jr. is known as a highly gifted actor, but also as a person who went through a long range of substance abuse related arrests and incarcerations. These encounters with the law resulted at several stages in him being fired from promising projects, and even to the entire movie industry becoming leery to contract him anymore for new projects despite his brilliance on the screen.*[4]
> 
> *Downey started using drugs at the tender age of 6, having a father who was an actor and a drug addict. Using drugs together seemed to be the way Robert and his father bonded, but unfortunately, it also led to a turbulent youth with relocations and school dropouts, and later relational breakups, career setbacks, probations and incarcerations.*[5] *His career reached its lowest point when he was sentenced to three years prison in 1999 for violating parole from an earlier arrest. He was granted an early release and got cast in a recurring role on the television series Ally McBeal, for which he won a Golden Globe Award. Yet, his drug problems continued, and so did his recurring arrests.*[6]
> 
> *Thanks to the faith and support from some of his friends, particularly Mel Gibson, and his own deep contemplations as he shifted from exquisite hotel rooms to penitentiary cells, Downey vowed to release the habits that brought him contract losses, break ups, and a poor reputation. According to his own testimony, he has been drug-free since 2003, thanks to the help of his wife, therapy, meditation, recovery programs, yoga, and kung fu. He explained that the hardest part of rehabilitating and pursuing newness is not the act, but the decision to do it. Thanks to his re-discovered stability, Robert Downey Jr. has evolved into one of the most respected actors in Hollywood with an impressive list of credits to his name.*[7]

Robert Downey jr. has been fortunate to be granted multiple chances in life, but then again, this is the case with most of us. There is always a window that opens when a door closes, but we sometimes miss that because we keep staring at the closed door, and overlook the fact that newness also comes with

---

[4] Robert Downey Jr. (Sept. 16, 2022). *Biography.com*. Retrieved from https://www.biography.com/actors/robert-downey-jr
[5] Robert Downey Jr. Bio. *IMDB*. Retrieved from https://www.imdb.com/name/nm0000375/bio/
[6] Cunningham, J. M. (Dec. 17, 2023). Robert Downey Jr.—Actor. *Encyclopedia Britannica*. Retrieved from https://www.britannica.com/biography/Robert-Downey-Jr
[7] Robert Downey Jr. Bio. *IMDB*. Retrieved from https://www.imdb.com/name/nm0000375/bio/

different paths. What may have been Downey's greatest blessings were his friends, his wife, and his gravitation to meditation and deep contemplation. He declares himself a Jewish Buddhist (JUBU) but seems to equally honor other religious affiliations.[8] And while it is great that Downey had a support system, it should be underscored that it was ultimately his own willpower and determination—his choice—that elevated him past the recurring relapses into a world of balanced and gratifying newness.

*Ursula Burns is the first African American women to have been the CEO of a Fortune 500 company. She was the daughter of Panamanian immigrants and raised by a single mother in a New York City housing project. Her mother operated a home day-care center and took ironing and cleaning jobs to earn money to pay for her schooling.[9] Upon earning a Bachelor of Science degree in mechanical engineering, she became a summer intern at Xerox in 1980, an opportunity that granted her the experience and financial means to pursue a Master of Science degree at Columbia University through a minority supporting initiative.*

*Once she earned her Masters degree, Ursula continued working at Xerox in a variety of positions for 10 years before being offered a job as executive assistant. From there on, she rose the ranks in various executive positions, eventually making it to senior vice president of corporate strategic services in May 2000. She developed a mutually rewarding relationship with then-CEO Anne Mulcahy, who invited her to become president of business group operations. Seven years later, Burns assumed the role of president, and in 2009 she was named CEO, succeeding Mulcahy. Burns subsequently led Xerox through various strategic evolutions, some of which very tense, until she stepped down from the position in December 2016.*

*In addition to her groundbreaking roles at Xerox, Burns also served on the board of directors of multiple large American companies, including Uber, American Express, and ExxonMobil. From 2009 to 2016, President Barack Obama assigned her leadership of the White House national program on Science, Technology, Engineering, and Math (STEM), while she also served as Chairwoman of the President's Export Council from 2015 to 2016.[10] From 2017 through 2020, Burns served as chairman and later CEO of VEON, the world's 11th largest telecom service provider by subscribers. Thanks to her stellar performance, Ms. Burns was listed multiple times by Forbes as one of the 100 most powerful women in the world.*

---

[8] De Vries, H. (November 21, 2004). "Robert Downey Jr.: The Album". *The New York Times*. Archived from the original on April 22, 2012. Retrieved January 1, 2024.
[9] Nolan, J. L. (Sept. 16, 2023). Ursula Burns—American Executive. *Encyclopedia Britannica*. Retrieved from https://www.britannica.com/biography/Ursula-Burns
[10] Ursula Burns—Executive Chairman, VEON. Forbes. Retrieved from https://www.forbes.com/profile/ursula-burns/?sh=63ed75e340a0

Ursula Burns has experienced her share of discrimination in and outside of the professional world. Looking back at her years at Xerox she admits that the company broke some ground in the 80's, but she realized, as she rose into executive positions, that race and gender were still issues. As an example, she mentioned that people often told her how amazing she was, and only later she realized that this was their way to justify her being a woman of color in her position.[11] In private life she has been aware of being followed in stores based on her skin color, even when she was already a highly paid executive.[12] Ms. Burns volunteers with organizations that support women toward obtaining knowledge and self-respect to take chances and pursue their aspirations. As examples, she offers leadership advice to FIRST, the National Academy Foundation, and the U.S. Olympic Committee.[13] Ursula Burns has seen both as she rose from humble beginnings to groundbreaking prominence, and made the *choice* to expand her awareness and growth by seizing every opportunity toward newness. It happened when she moved from the poverty she was brought up in to a rewarding career at Xerox, and then, when she had to step down due to strategic frictions, to other honorable positions. In her own words: "*Dreams do come true, but not without the help of others, a good education, a strong work ethic and the courage to lean in*".[14]

## Newness: The Path Toward Continuous Improvement

Newness is a choice. As you may have read from Gardner's earlier cited article, some people get stumped by life, and cease their efforts to propel into new opportunities. He explained that with a short quote about barnacles, which may be a powerful alert to all of us to re-tap into our inexhaustible well of energy and reinvent ourselves.

So, how did Robert Downey jr. and Ursula Burns deal with the elements of newness?

---

[11] Ignatius, A. (July–August 2021). "I'm Here Because I'm As Good As You." *Harvard Business Review*. Retrieved from https://hbr.org/2021/07/im-here-because-im-as-good-as-you

[12] Ibid.

[13] Ivery, K. (July 1, 2022). Ursula Burns Bio: The Inspiring Story of an Incredible Women. *Business Chronicler*. https://businesschronicler.com/business-bios/ursula-burns-bio/

[14] Lean In: Ursula Burns, Chairman & CEO. *Lean In*. Retrieved from https://leanin.org/stories/ursula-burns

## Self-Renewal

Robert Downey understood, after multiple arrests, incarcerations, and contract losses, that it was up to him to reset his modus operandi if he wanted his life to be worthwhile. Fortunately, he did so. Ursula Burns encountered multiple twists in her life and realized that she had to shift gears where needed to continue her path. When the strategic split at Xerox went awry, she stepped down as the lead person, ended her task responsibly, and moved on.

## Inner Change

The inner change that Downey jr. underwent must have been a strong one, considering that he had been using drugs since he was 6 years old. One can only imagine what inner change was required when he finally decided that it was time to turn the pages. This act can only call for deep respect. Similarly, Burns has experienced numerous verbal and psychological violations as a black woman from humble beginnings, leading a Fortune 500 company. Yet, she choose to avoid bitterness, and took the high road rather than wasteful confrontation.

## Optimism

Both of the individuals described in this chapter demonstrated a healthy dose of optimism in shifting gears repeatedly in their life toward the place they achieved in history. Had they not been optimistic, they would have most likely given up on themselves long ago, based on the statistics that were against them: how many addicts to hard drugs find the inner strength to radically change? How many poor persons of color muster the courage and stamina to defy all odds to become a Fortune-500 CEO?

## Open-Mindedness

Both, Downey jr. and Burns kept an open mind regarding the options in their future. They may not have expected the outcomes to be as rosy as they did, but they were willing to give their best, and their best turned out to be good enough.

## Meaning

*Meaning is not something you stumble across, like the answer to a riddle or the prize in a treasure hunt. Meaning is something you build into your life. You build it out of your own past, out of your affections and loyalties, out of the experience of humankind as it is passed on to you, out of your own talent and understanding, out of the things you believe in, out of the things and people you love, out of the values for which you are willing to sacrifice something.*[15]

Considering Gardner's excellent explanation about meaning here above, we can only conclude that both, Robert Downey jr. and Ursula Burns built meaning in their life, reflecting on their pasts, looking at their future, and based on the sacrifices they were willing to make.

> Point to Ponder
>
> Between self-renewal, inner-change, optimism, open-mindedness, and meaning: please rank the quality or behavior you consider most strongly represented in you?
> Share an example how you were able to apply the selected strength?
> Now, consider the quality or behavior you need to work on.
> Share an example where you could have used this skill and did not?

Figure 7.1 above shows the actions and behaviors you will most likely come across when you practice newness based on the circumstances you encounter. The different colors of the elements, which should not be seen as the only important elements in the internalizing process, reflect the intensity of each. In Fig. 7.1, I chose to grant inner change the darker color, as it is the most intense, and oftentimes downright the most difficult, process in the cycle. Optimism, open-mindedness, and meaning, are behaviors that could be challenging at first, but can become recurring traits and therefore easier to apply if you keep them intact. Self-renewal, finally, is a wonderful consequence of all the mental and emotional work invested in yourself, and will usually lead to bright outcomes.

---

[15] Gardner, J. (November 10, 1990). *Personal Renewal by John Gardner*. Delivered to McKinsey & Company, Phoenix, AZ. Retrieved from https://fs.blog/great-talks/personal-renewal-john-gardner/

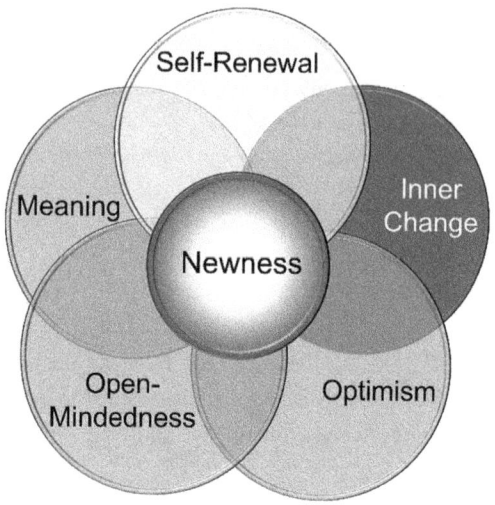

**Fig. 7.1** Newness

- *Inner change* is the challenging step you face when external changes appear, or when you find that the path you have been on is not rewarding, or even destructive. It takes a lot of courage to make the choice to engage in inner change, and it will take all the help and determination you can conjure inside. As Robert Downey jr. revealed, he has been meditating, doing yoga, kung fu, and more to establish and maintain the inner change he wanted to establish. It's an ongoing process, but can be a very rewarding one, and every subsequent time you face the requirement for inner change, it will become easier to do.

To dive a little deeper into the reasons why you may want to engage in inner change: I found an article that presented a list of such reasons you may have:

- Changing your attitude toward people and life.
- Becoming a more positive person.
- Becoming more optimistic.
- Becoming a kinder and more tolerant person.
- Developing your willpower and your self-discipline.
- Awakening motivation.
- Overcoming negative habits and building positive habits.[16]

---

[16] Sasson, R. (ND). How and Why Inner Changes Create External Changes. Success Consciousness. https://www.successconsciousness.com/blog/personal-development/making-inner-change/

The same article also elaborated on possible actions that might follow if you would start following some self-improvement techniques:

- Your new thoughts and attitude could bring new expectations and hopes and change how you view your outer world.
- The inner changes within you would gradually affect your outer life.
- Your behavior and how you act would change, affecting your relationships favorably, how people would treat you, and the experiences you would undergo.
- You would attract new opportunities in various areas of your life.
- You would have more energy, ambition, and inner strength.
- You would get over your fear of change and be ready to take action, change, and improve your life according to the changes happening within you.[17]

These are all appealing shifts in your life that may be worth considering.
- *Optimism* is yet another internal phenomenon that is not always readily available. Remember, sometimes blessings come disguised as curses vice versa. It's therefore wise to contemplate over several days, weeks even, to land in a place where you can perceive a situation you are dealing with from an optimistic angle. You may need the help of a mentor, friend, partner, or other to help you evaluate and re-evaluate, but remember, there is always an optimistic way to look at matters. If not in the situation itself, then perhaps in what you can do afterwards, or how you can help others in similar situations later.

There is a lot to say about optimism, even if this section was not included. Unless you are a habitual pessimist, which I don't hope, you most likely experienced the power of optimism. But let's look what others wrote about it. The author of the article I'm about to cite here interviewed a molecular biologist and author by the name of John Medina. Medina's research established that we live far beyond our ancestors, many of whom did not make it to 30! Our brain is at its peak around 24 years, and after that, it starts eroding. So, it's imperative that we do something to halt the decline process, and this is where optimism comes in. Even brain scientists seem to agree that a positive attitude will help you live longer and be a better leader.

If you have a "glass is half full" attitude, you also deal better with depression, as it will have a harder time getting a grip on you. Depression attacks your immune system, and can lead to not only mental but also physical ailments. Optimism also increases the production of dopamine, which acts on areas of the brain to give you feelings of pleasure, satisfaction and motivation.

---

[17] Ibid.

The article cited here also shared two powerful suggestions to boost your optimism through an increased sense of gratitude (which I discussed in the previous chapter). The suggestions are:

1. The Gratitude Visit: This is where you write a 300-word letter to someone who means a lot to you. Visit this person and read the letter out loud to them. The positive vibes will linger with you for a week or longer.
2. Three Good Things: Here is where you consider, at the end of every day, three good things that happened. Write them down, along with why they happened. The effect of this exercise will work wonders for your belief in the good things of life, hence, your optimism.[18]

- *Open-mindedness* is also a delicate matter, because you may not always be aware that you are closed minded about certain issues. We all grow up with biases and develop mental models to define quick opinions on the things we encounter. Then, when it's time for newness, we may not be aware that we need to recalibrate our perspectives. Talking to a trusted and honest friend, mentor or teacher can take you a long way, and meditation can also be a great insight enhancer.

In recent decades the importance of open-mindedness has been strongly emphasized. There are multiple reasons at the foundation of this trend: we experience more change, our workplaces have more diversity, which means that we have to learn to work with people who may not be at the same wavelength with our perspectives, and there have been too many sources pointing out how detrimental closed-mindedness can be for your progress.

Management researchers have found that open-mindedness encourages the receptiveness to learn. In workplaces, managers who are open-minded continuously search for ways to improve processes and productions in order to spearhead advancement. And because they know that great ideas often house in other people's heads, they gladly keep communication lines open to learn from their co-workers, so that there can be frequent sharing of ideas, suggestions and views.

This desire to learn from others and share ideas also induces humility, as it enhances the insight that we should respect others and encourage them to establish an inclusive environment and cultivate team spirit. People with an open mind will be less prone to resist change in their organizations, because they understand that this is usually the way toward innovation.[19]

---

[18] Gallo, C. (Nov. 19, 2017). Brain Science Reveals the Striking Power of Optimism. Forbes. Retrieved from https://www.forbes.com/sites/carminegallo/2017/11/19/brain-science-reveals-the-striking-power-of-optimism/?sh=4cb215de71aa

[19] Al-Abrrow, H., Akram, S. F., Abdullah, H., Khaw, K. W., Alnoor, A., & Rexhepi, G. (2023). Effect of open-mindedness and humble behavior on innovation: Mediator role of learning. *International Journal of Emerging Markets, 18*(9), 3065–3084.

– *Meaning* is what you attribute to the things you encounter and how you want them to affect your life. Your values often come into play when you determine the meaning that something, someone, or a situation has for you. It is important to regularly ask yourself what the meaning is of the path you are on, and if you consider it meaningful enough.

Meaning in life can be a huge motivator in moving ahead. Victor Frankl, who wrote "Man's Search for Meaning", underscored that the strongest motivational force in humans is a will to meaning.[20] Indeed: having a sense of meaning in your life is essential to your psychological well-being.[21]

The fascinating part of meaning in life is, however, that its contents will differ from one person to another. In other words, meaning in your life is what *you* say it is. A good way to determine your life's meaning is to obtain clarity about who you are, where you feel you belong, and what you want to accomplish with your life.[22] When you feel that your life is meaningful, you are motivated to address the challenges in your life, because you are aware of the ultimate goal. So, the path toward making meaning, and the content of meaning are both subjective phenomena, determined by you as the person who interprets them.

Keep in mind that meaning is not limited to just one area of your life. Most people also want to find meaning in their work, since they spend so much time there. In fact, research has proven that many people don't mind taking a pay cut if that means that their work will become more meaningful to them. You should also know that when you consider your work meaningful, there is a major chance that you will also feel that your life in general is meaningful.[23] This can be explained by the fact that work holds a central role in your life. If you feel that what you do for your livelihood is meaningful, you are more fulfilled, and also more willing to contribute, where possible, to the wellness of the stakeholders in your workplace, and to society as a whole.[24]

– *Self-Renewal* is the continuous process that you undergo, even when you are not aware of it. However, when you encounter major changes, such as a change of job or career, a divorce or marriage, birth or death, moving to another city, state, or country, you become more aware of the need to

---

[20] Frankl, V. E. (1984). *Man's Search for Meaning* (Revised and updated). Washington Square Press.

[21] Bailey, C., & Madden, A. (2019). 'We're not scum, we're human': Agential responses in the face of meaningless work. *Scandinavian Journal of Management, 35*(4), 101064.

[22] Steger, M. F., Kashdan, T. B., Sullivan, B. A., & Lorentz, D. (2008). Understanding the search for meaning in life: Personality, cognitive style, and the dynamic between seeking and experiencing meaning. Journal of Personality, 72(2), 199–228.

[23] Allan, B. A., Autin, K. L., & Duffy, R. D. (2014). Examining social class and work meaning within the psychology of working framework. *Journal of Career Assessment, 22*(4), 543–561.

[24] de Klerk, J. J. (2023). Searching for meaning in a disruptive world – constructing a lexicon of the meanings of meaning. *SA Journal of Industrial Psychology, 49*

engage in self-renewal. That is when the factors described in Fig. 7.1 become useful.

Tony Robbins, famous motivational speaker, presented a very sensible set of actions you could consider to engage in self-renewal. Self-renewal ensures your personal growth, and helps you keep your focus on your life's purpose. Self-renewal is an essential part of our spiritual wellness. I selected five of the 11 suggestions here, and invite you to visit the website to read the rest.

- Take a break: Keeping your nose to the grindstone is a diligent endeavor, but if you can unplug now and then, you may see a lot more and refocus on the biggest picture of your purpose.
- Improve your self-awareness: you need to figure out what you truly want, and you can only do that through deep contemplation. You cannot accomplish this major piece of insight into yourself if you don't open your mind's eyes and see yourself for who you really are.
- Formulate your purpose: this also came up in the point about meaning above, as well as in other sections of this book. Deciding on your purpose is critical to know where you want to go, and what you need to do. Once you know your purpose, you can connect your goal to it.
- Scrutinize your self-perspectives: What are the mental models that limit you from going all the way to where you want to go? This has been brought up earlier as well. Take a hard look at your beliefs and see what needs to be renewed there. Holding on to limiting perspectives will keep you from truly renewing yourself.
- Dare to get out of your comfort zone. Reach out to other people than the ones you always hang out with. This will expand your horizon and bring you new insights. Do things you normally don't do. Learn a new sport, language, or instrument. Exposure to newness conjures more newness in very surprising ways. People you wouldn't normally interact with. Learn a new language or instrument.[25]

## Chapter Highlights

- *Newness* is something you experience from day to day, and even throughout the day. Every experience you go through, everything you witness or learn, infuses new insights in you, and enhances your perspectives. You can for-

---

[25] Robbins, T. (ND). How to Renew Yourself. *Productivity & Performance.* Retrieved from https://www.tonyrobbins.com/productivity-performance/renew-yourself/#:~:text=Self%2Drenewal%20is%20an%20essential,and%20rediscover%20your%20true%20spirit

give yourself today because you are no longer the person you were yesterday. Thanks to internalizing yesterday's lesson, you have become a new person.
- *Apoptosis is the biological explanation for newness.* It entails the death of cells, which occurs as a normal and controlled part of an organism's growth or development.
- *Life offers each of us so many changes to improve and grow*, thanks to our ability to internalize, and then change. These instances of repeated renewal can be defined as our continuous rebirths. And because we have the ability to think things over and adjust our behavior based on that, we can renew ourselves whenever we want to.
- *Renewal* is a religious process. You don't have to be religious in any way to experience newness.
- *Newness is a choice.*

  - *Inner change* is the challenging step you face when external changes appear, or when you find that the path you have been on is not rewarding, or even destructive. It takes a lot of courage to make the choice to engage in inner change, and it will take all the help and determination you can conjure inside.
  - *Optimism* is yet another internal phenomenon that is not always readily available. Remember, sometimes blessings come disguised as curses vice versa. Contemplate over several days, weeks even, to land in a place where you can perceive a situation you are dealing with from an optimistic angle.
  - *Open-mindedness* is also a tricky thing, because you may not always be aware that you are closed minded about some things.
  - *Meaning* is what you attribute to the things you encounter and how you want them to affect your life. Your values often come into play when you determine the meaning that something, someone, or a situation has for you.
  - *Self-Renewal* is the continuous process that we undergo, even when we are not aware of it.

# 8

# Practices and Exercises Supporting GAIN

**Contents**
Celebrating GAIN .................................................................................................. 100
The Noble Eightfold Path ...................................................................................... 106
Chapter Highlights ................................................................................................ 110

**Abstract** This chapter discusses some exercises that can help in practicing GAIN. Journaling, yoga, and observation practices are some of the suggestions to be made. It will also briefly discuss the Noble Eightfold Path, which is an ancient strategy to ending suffering. This path consists of a combination of eight constructive practices: Right understanding, Right thought, Right speech, Right action, Right livelihood, Right effort, Right mindfulness, and Right concentration. Each of these practices will briefly be explained with an emphasis on their interconnectedness.

**The Mindfulness of the Banana Tree: A Story**
One day an angry and wild wind entered a quiet village. It blew with near-hurricane fierce over the mountains and through the streets, ripping branches and uprooting some of the oldest, strongest trees in the area, blowing off parts of roofs from homes, and keeping everybody grounded in fear for what might happen if one would take to the streets.

When the wind finally dissipated, the villagers came out to assess the damage the wind had done. Much to their surprise, the two banana trees from aunt Leila were still standing—unharmed!

The people were amazed and so were the plants and the animals! One of the large trees who had lost quite some of its branches, asked the banana trees what their secret to sustaining themselves was. The banana trees responded: "Well, nimbleness and flexibility first, and right mindfulness to go with the flow rather than trying to use counter force. The wind was upset, and the worst to do in such a case is trying to stand your ground at that time. There will be ample opportunities later to make your point. That's what we're doing now: we remained unscathed".

> Sometimes the best gain is to lose.[1]
>
> ~George Herbert

## Celebrating GAIN

It takes some mental adjustment to perceive every occurrence in your life as GAIN. Since you are subject to moods and emotions, you can sometimes feel defeated by unexpected surprises that turn your comfortable world upside down. Even if your comfortable world is far from perfect, you may have accepted it for what it is, just like so many of us do.

To briefly resume the GAIN cycle in light of your daily activities:

- *Generating* is the process of experiencing things. As indicated in Chap. 3, whether you are aware of it or not, and whether it is your intention or not, you are constantly generating new "dots" (experiences) to connect in the future. The one thing that will become clear as you progress in life is that no experience is wasted, and that everything serves a purpose in hindsight. Just like a puzzle, the pieces fall in place, even if it may take many years before that happens.
- *Appreciating* is the consequence of perceiving every experience as a valuable dot in the greater scheme of your life. When nothing is wasted, everything is worth appreciating, no matter how strange that sometimes may feel. Remember the statements from Epictetus and Victor Frankl, two men living thousands of years apart, yet coming to the same conclusion, which is that you control your attitude toward anything that happens. While our interpretation of anything often depends on our mood at the moment, we can still reflect at the end of every day, and sometimes several days or weeks later, to develop a wholesome perspective of what happened.

---

[1] https://www.brainyquote.com/quotes/george_herbert_379990?src=t_gain

- *Internalizing* entails the process of deeply contemplating the occurrences. When you internalize, you turn inward for intense reflection, and consider the things that happened in their deeper setting. Something that occurred recently may represent a repeating pattern in your life, which clearly indicates that there is a lesson to be learned. The internalization process can provide answers on changes you may have to implement in your work, home, or other areas, so that the "teacher of this recurring lesson" may disappear.
- *Newness* is the change that you bring about in yourself based on the generating, appreciating, and internalizing practice. Newness is the result of mindful transformation that usually reveals improvement in your approaches.

What follows below is an overview of some of the easiest ways to make the GAIN experience useful. Keep in mind that not every one of these approaches may appeal to you, but hopefully some will.

1. Meditation

    I have mentioned meditation often enough in this book to confirm that I strongly believe in this practice as a calming, healing, and insight evoking one. It's particularly the insight that results from meditation, whether it is your intention or not, that makes it a wonderful practice. You don't have to meditate for hours in a row, but if you can reserve 10 to 15 minutes a day to sit calmly, relax, and focus on your breathing, the rest usually comes automatically. If sitting in the lotus position doesn't come easy to you, it's not a problem. You can meditate in any position. You can even engage in walking or driving meditation. Just make sure you don't close your eyes while doing that. But the focus on your breathing does wonders for your psyche. There are many guided meditation videos available on YouTube. Pick one that appeals to you and start using it. You will not obtain bliss from the exercise, but a deep calmness and a sense of gratitude may result from it, helping you to see that life is really GAIN.

2. Long relaxing walks

    Walking is by default a healthy practice, and it has been proven that it does not only bring physical benefits, but also mental ones. While you walk, you can let your thoughts run freely, and get some great insights. I have used walking as a catalyst for new ideas. Many of the books and papers I wrote are the result from an insight that emerged while I walked. Sometimes I did so with my dog, and sometimes I would do it alone. If you walk with someone else, that's nice too, but you will not have a chance to engage in a deep inner search if you also have to make conversation. That said, a long walk with a mentor, or to talk about something you need help with, may be just as therapeutic as walking alone. Make sure you choose safe, nice places, so that your eyes can enjoy the scenery. And while you may take your mobile phone with you, try to refrain from texting or talking with someone on the phone while you enjoy your rejuvenating, inspiring walk. You should not underestimate the powerful influence of a scenic impression: the beauty of the trees, the tweet of birds, the smell of spring, a gentle breeze: nature is a great facilitator of the insight that life is really GAIN.

3. Yoga

Yoga is the collective phrase for a group of physical, mental, and spiritual practices or disciplines that can help you control and quieten the mind. It is an ancient practice that involves physical poses, concentration, and deep breathing.[2] Yoga doesn't exclude anyone, so it is not only for flexible and fit people, as you may have seen on television or in magazines. Yoga can be done by any person, young, old, flexible or not, healthy or not. It can be very relaxing and even healing. And while yoga is practiced in various religions, it is not a religious practice per se. There are various forms of yoga that invite for various practices. Yoga is a systematic technology to improve the body, understand the mind, and free the spirit. Yoga can result in flexibility, strength, energy, and a more youthful appearance. It strengthens and calms your nervous system, increases the blood flow, and brings more oxygen to your cells.[3] Suggestions for yoga exercises are widely available on the Net, and a good place to find an appealing form of yoga practicing can be found in Medical New Today.[4] The wonderful practice of yoga may help you realize that life is really GAIN.

4. Change of environment

Stepping away from the daily routine is a refreshing way of rejuvenating your vision on life. You don't necessarily have to go abroad or stay away for days or weeks to enjoy this mental treat. A simple road trip to a neighboring town or village can do the trick for you. It's just about exposing yourself to a different environment, seeing different people and

---

[2] Nichols, H. (April 26, 2023). How does Yoga Work? (2024). *Medical News Today*. Retrieved from https://www.medicalnewstoday.com/articles/286745#what-is-yoga

[3] McCall, T. (2024). What Yoga is and what it Isn't. *Omega Institute for Holistic Studies*. Retrieved from https://www.eomega.org/article/what-yoga-is-what-it-isnt?gclid=Cj0KCQiAhc-sBhCEARIsAOVwHuSvPfbknwNhT-JEXjXNlY3NZxCnWkbTkfKBl3RaRz1kBBRErxwuiQMaAoPuEALw_wcB

[4] Martin, L. (July 9, 2021). How does yoga affect the body, and how can someone start practicing yoga?. *Medical News Today*. Retrieved from https://www.medicalnewstoday.com/articles/yoga-exercises

things, and releasing yourself from the status quo. Staying in the same place and having the same old routine can be depressing, especially when things don't look too bright. Exposing yourself to a different place can do wonders for your mental outlook, and infuse new energy and fresh perspectives in your mind. Sometimes it's the change of environment that you need to realize that life is really GAIN.

5. Watching a good movie

A good movie is not the same thing for everyone. If you go for this option of supporting your insights, follow your own preference. The good news is that we can get to view most movies at home with the right cable or satellite package. Some of us may prefer to physically attend a local cinema, and that has its own charm as well. It's a way to be away from home or work, and treat yourself on an outing. While there is no guarantee that the movie will provide you the answers to your immediate problems, it may distract you enough from your concerns, and even bring you in a more constructive mental state, which will in turn induce renewed brain energy to look at things in a different light, and realize that life is truly GAIN.

6. Journaling

Journaling has been described as a great solution for many struggles. By journaling, you basically become your own healer, as you write your experiences, and when reading them back, you may find the answers you did not know you knew! Journaling reveals the inner source of wisdom you carry with you and can bring you deep insights in what really troubles you, and how best to address it. This is how you may also realize, then, that life is truly GAIN.

7. Reading

There are billions of books and articles available, and not just in bookstores. You can find uplifting and insightful on this beautiful gift called the Internet! If you're not an intense reader, you can limit yourself to short reading pieces, but know this: by reading you allow your mind to take a peak in another world (just like with movies), and release the stress that caused a somber mind or a sense of hopelessness. I recently bought a book on Zen stories. I love Zen stories. Whenever I feel the need to, I just open it at any random page and read a story. I am finding that I always encounter a piece of useful advice in the story, and feel strengthened to face the day with new energy. Try to discover what material you prefer to read and treat yourself to that. It may help you realize that life is truly GAIN.

8. Connecting with a sounding board

    I decided to use "sounding board" instead of "mentor", because you may very well have a great friend, neighbor, or family member with whom you can talk about deep subjects, and from whom you can receive some great insights. Some of us have mentors, and those are always great to have, but remember that mentors come and go in your life. Mentors are human beings too, and while they may be a great asset at one stage in your life, they may not be in another. If you are fortunate enough to identify a sounding board who wants to take the time to listen and provide constructive feedback, you will get great satisfaction from this relationship, and experience that life is really GAIN.

9. Reframing

    This may not be the easiest practice, but it could be helpful to those who want to try it. Reframing means that you change your mindset about something you are going through, and try to analyze it from a different angle. The point is that your first impression of something you encounter may be negative, based on your biases and the mental models you built in our mind. This is sometimes also referred to as distortion—a negative and sometimes even irrational thought process), and it needs cognitive restructuring to bring matters back in perspective. Distortions can lead to depression, poor decisions, and other negative results, so that would be your cue to engage in cognitive restructuring. Reframing may be positively influenced by meditation and certain yoga practices.

10. Become a member of a contemplative circle.

    The world has been enriched by numerous in-person and online groups, which you can find through your connections or on social media. There are groups for like-minded people based on practically any criterion you can think of: religion, intellectual, psychological, philosophical, practice-based, skill-based, medically-focused, and more. Finding such a group that you can become part of may be very therapeutic. Of course you can also contact a therapist with whom you can establish weekly consultation meetings toward personal improvement. These options of constructive human interaction can help you realize that life is truly GAIN.

> **Point to Ponder**
>
> After reading the ten suggested approaches in support of the GAIN experience, please rank the practices from most appealing to least appealing to you?

Is there one or more you have tries, and if so, what were your general findings regarding their influence on your mindset?

Which of these practices have you not tried yet but would you like to try, and how could you go about it?

**Our Common Ground**

There are no two moments alike
In this capricious journey of life
Ebbs and flows continuously strike
On this breathtaking, backbreaking hike
We so often fill with senseless strife

The art of living is no secret to us
We've been around long enough
We know that there's no fulfilment in fuss
It feels like riding in the wrong bus
On a road that's winding and rough

Yet, while all lessons were previously taught
We prefer to repeat old mistakes
The human path is inexplicably fraught
Through choices we make – promises we break
And directions we valiantly decide to take
Until by a surprising end we get caught…

What are we chasing, may I ask?
How do we perceive our personal trail?
What is, in the end, our critical task?
And what are we hiding behind our mask?
Are we the hammer and is life our nail?

Acquiring peace is a personal choice
Regardless of the turmoil around
We can find tranquility amidst noise
Discover our inner peace-loving poise
And make mutual acceptance our common ground

*–Joan Marques*

# The Noble Eightfold Path

What follows below is not a call for any religious conversion. It is a brief overview of one of the foundational thoughts and practices in Buddhist psychology (again—not to be confused with religion), which has made important advances in the Eastern and Western world over the past decades. The Noble Eightfold Path is an ancient concept that derives from the Buddhist insight of the Four Noble truths.

So, what are these truths? Very simple: Truth 1. Suffering exists; Truth 2: Suffering has a cause; Truth 3: Suffering can be ended; and Truth 4: This can happen through the Noble Eightfold Path (see Fig. 8.1 below).

It may be useful to clarify that suffering may be an insufficient term. It doesn't necessarily mean pain and misery, but more the fact that we often struggle with dissatisfactions, either because we want something we cannot get, or because we want to get rid of something we cannot release. That "something" can be anything: a relationship, a job, a car, a beautiful home, peace of mind, wealth, you just name it.

So, now that we have established that the Four Noble Truths make good common sense, let's see what the way to liberate ourselves from suffering

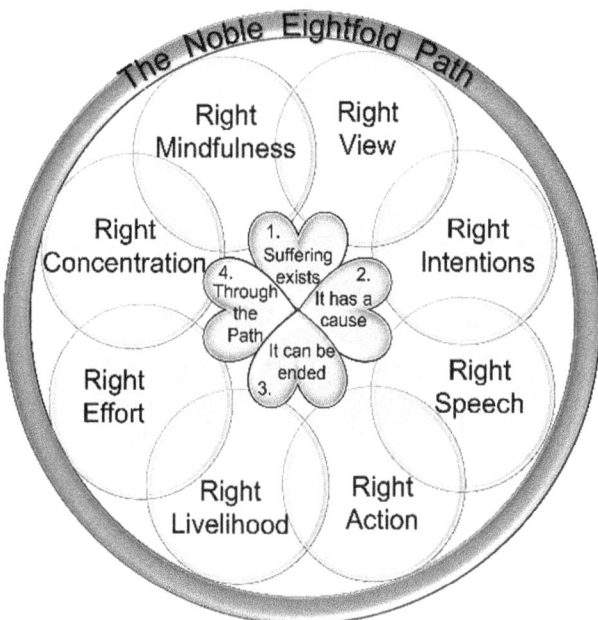

**Fig. 8.1** The Noble Eightfold Path

entails. The Noble Eightfold Path, which is the fourth noble truth, encompasses the following practices or insights: Right View; Right Intention; Right Speech; Right Action; Right Livelihood; Right Effort; Right Mindfulness; and Right Concentration. There is no specific sequence in this set of insights, because they are interrelated.

For practical reasons, let us start with the first-mentioned insight and take it from there:

*Right view* entails your ability to scrutinize which of your mindsets are constructive and nourish those. It also influences your perception: how you consider the things that happen to and around you. You can either maintain a negative view and perceive everything as an attack to the quality of life, or decide to look at things from a positive angle and distinguish the positive lessons in each experience. Right view adjusts limiting perspectives, and may even lead us to understand that actually, all perspectives are limiting. Thus, right view influences your attitude (think of the statements from Epictetus and Victor Frankl's cited earlier about attitude).

*Right intention*, sometimes also referred to as "right thinking," pertains to your mental focus. Maintaining a right intention is not as easy as it may seem. Thich Nhat Hanh, who used to be world's most famous Zen Buddhist, recommended four actions to refrain from losing right intention: (1) Ensuring proper understanding of what you see, read or hear, and contemplate on things first, since first impressions may be misleading; (2) Scrutinizing your actions in order to verify that you are not mindlessly exerting adopted habits, but engage in well-considered behavior; (3) Inspecting your habits, and acknowledging that you have good and bad ones. Knowing your bad habits can help you refrain from allowing them to emerge at times when you least need them, and (4) Nurturing an awakened mind in order to benefit others as much as possible. In Buddhism this is referred to as "Bodhicitta." When you engage in Bodhicitta, you become filled with the intention to do well onto others and help them become happier beings.[5]

*Right Speech* has become a prominent concern in our current day and age, filled with massive, multiple communication avenues. Words are important means of information sharing, and they can be constructive or destructive. Engaging in right speech entails that you deliberate refrain from saying things that negatively affect others. It further entails that you practice mindfulness when you share information that has not been verified and

---

[5] Marques, J. (2021). *Leading with Awareness*. Routledge (Taylor & Francis), New York, NY.

could be harmful to other parties. Right speech means telling the truth to the best of your abilities, not creating divisiveness by telling different people different things, refraining from making cruel statements, and refraining from overstatements.[6]

*Right Action* is best implemented when you end destructive practices, including the action of harming yourself and others. Right action should be broadly interpreted, and it requires a careful examination of your behavior. Right action points at the protection of life, and the preservation of wellbeing of all living creatures in the broadest sense possible. In Buddhist circles, right action consists of three main considerations: no killing, no stealing, no sexual misconduct. Looking deeper into this, it really means no killing (of any living being), no stealing, no insulting, no lying, no cheating, no backbiting, no harsh words, no manipulating, no mean-spirited thoughts, or behavior, and not engaging in any type of misconduct.

*Right Livelihood* pertains to the ways people earn their living. It predominantly focuses on the nature of the work you do, and whether this is constructive or not. Thich Nhat Hanh[7] suggests some of the critical questions you could reflect on to ensure that you practice right and not wrong livelihood, such as, (a) whether you are producing, dealing in, or promoting weapons of any kind that are being used to kill and destroy; (b) whether you are engaging in practices where people are blatantly being taken advantage of, or (c) whether you are involved in the production and/or promotion of destructive products such as alcohol and drugs.

*Right Effort*, which is also referred to as "right diligence", is a very deliberate act. While effort is generally an admirable practice, it can be directed to constructive or destructive activities. People who work in industries that produce items for destruction undeniably invest effort in their job. Unfortunately, this cannot be considered right effort, due to the suffering it causes. Right effort, like all other treads of the eightfold path, requires careful evaluation of our actions, thoughts, and intentions, in order to assess whether they are constructive. Similar to the other elements of the path, right effort is very personal in nature as well. It should be applied as a way of contemplating on the roots of your suffering, and subsequently engaging in the effort to release those roots.

---

[6] Thich, N. H. (1998). *The Heart of the Buddha's Teaching: Transforming Suffering into Peace, Joy, and Liberation*. Broadway Books, New York, NY.

[7] Thich, N. H. (1998). *The Heart of the Buddha's Teaching: Transforming Suffering into Peace, Joy, and Liberation*. Broadway Books, New York, NY.

*Right Mindfulness* encompasses the practice of all other facets of the eightfold path: right view, right intention, right speech, right action, right livelihood, right effort, and right concentration. When you are mindful, you see things that you usually take for granted: the grass, the trees, your partner, your colleagues, your pet, and you realize fully that they are here now. It is your mindfulness that can guide you toward truly appreciating what you see and displaying your gratitude for their presence. Through your mindfulness, you may activate the mindfulness of others. The appreciation that is part of mindfulness can relieve the suffering of mindlessness, and encourage you to go a step further, so that you concentrate on others, understand them better, and transform your own suffering and theirs into joy.[8]

*Right concentration* is also firmly intertwined with the other elements of the Noble Eightfold Path. It is oftentimes also referred to as Right Meditation. Right mindfulness and concentration are both tools to sharpen the mind,[9] which can be amplified through mindfulness or insight meditation, also known as Vipassana. Concentration is required to be present wherever you are. Once you can attain that, you will enjoy each moment to the fullest, and cease your excessive concerns about the past or the future. Through right concentration you can discover beautiful scenes that used to escape you when you were not concentrating. Right concentration can therefore lead you to greater happiness, since you are more focused on what matters now. If you engage deep enough in right concentration, you will ultimately start realizing the impermanent nature of many of your cravings, and learn to release them[10] (Thich, 1998).

A critical point to underscore again here is the fact that the elements of the Noble Eightfold Path are interrelated and inspire one another. An interpretation of implementing the Noble Eightfold Path could thus be as follows: if you engage in (morally) right view, you will mindfully concentrate on decisions that are based on improvement of the quality of life for all other living beings. Consequently, all your intention, communication (speech), effort, and actions will be geared toward the goal of behaving morally sound. With such a mindful approach from initial views to ultimate actions, you will become aware of the need to engage in right livelihood, as you consistently gauge your accomplishments to the high moral standards developed.

---

[8] Ibid.
[9] Nouri, D. (May 3, 2013). What is the Eightfold Path? *Secular Buddhist Association.* Retrieved from http://secularbuddhism.org/2013/05/03/what-is-the-eightfold-path/
[10] Thich, N. H. (1998). *The Heart of the Buddha's Teaching: Transforming Suffering into Peace, Joy, and Liberation.* Broadway Books, New York, NY.

> **Point to Ponder**
>
> Which of the eight elements of the Noble Eightfold Path comes easiest to you? If more than one, please mention and explain why?
> Which of the eight elements seems to be most difficult to practice?
> How could you improve practicing this element?

## Chapter Highlights

- *Resuming the GAIN cycle in light of your daily activities:*

  - *Generating* is the process of experiencing things. No experience is wasted. Everything serves a purpose in hindsight. Just like a puzzle, the pieces fall in place, even if it may take many years before that happens.
  - *Appreciating* is the consequence of perceiving every experience as a valuable dot in the greater scheme of your life. When nothing is wasted, everything is worth appreciating, no matter how strange that sometimes may feel.
  - Internalizing entails the process of deeply contemplating the occurrences. When you internalize, you turn inward for intense reflection, and consider the things that happened in their deeper setting.
  - Newness is the change that you bring about in yourself based on the generating, appreciating, and internalizing practice. Newness is the result of mindful transformation that usually reveals improvement in your approaches.

- *Overview of some of the easiest ways to make the GAIN experience useful:*

  - *Meditation:* You don't have to meditate for hours in a row, but if you can reserve 10–15 minutes a day to sit calmly, relax, and focus on your breathing, the rest usually comes automatically. There are many guided meditation videos available on YouTube. Pick one that appeals to you and start using it. You will not obtain bliss from the exercise, but a deep calmness and a sense of gratitude may result from it, helping you to see that life is really GAIN.
  - *Long relaxing walks:* Walking is by default a healthy practice, and it has been proven that it does not only bring physical benefits, but also mental ones. While you walk, you can let your thoughts run freely, and get

some great insights. Don't underestimate the powerful influence of a scenic impression: the beauty of the trees, the tweet of birds, the smell of spring, a gentle breeze: nature is a great facilitator of the insight that life is really GAIN.
- *Yoga:* Yoga is an ancient practice that involves physical poses, concentration, and deep breathing. It can be very relaxing and even healing. There are various forms of yoga that invite for various practices. Yoga strengthens and calms your nervous system, increases the blood flow, and brings more oxygen to your cells.
- *Change of environment:* You don't necessarily have to go abroad or stay away for days or weeks to enjoy this mental treat. A simple road trip to a neighboring town or village can do the trick for you. It's just about exposing yourself to a different environment, seeing different people and things, and releasing yourself from the status quo. Sometimes it's the change of environment that you need to realize that life is really GAIN.
- *Watching a good movie:* If you go for this option of supporting your insights, follow your own preference. You can view most movies at home with the right cable or satellite package. While there is no guarantee that the movie will provide you the answers to your immediate problems, it may distract you enough from your concerns, and even bring you in a more constructive mental state, which will in turn induce renewed brain energy to look at things in a different light, and realize that life is truly GAIN.
- *Journaling:*. By journaling, you basically become your own healer, as you write your experiences, and when reading them back, you may find the answers you did not know you knew! Journaling reveals the inner source of wisdom you carry with you and can bring you deep insights in what really troubles you, and how best to address it. This is how you may also realize, then, that life is truly GAIN.
- *Reading:* If you're not an intense reader, you can limit yourself to short reading pieces, but know this: by reading you allow your mind to take a peak in another world (just like with movies), and release the stress that caused a somber mind or a sense of hopelessness. Try to discover what material you prefer to read and treat yourself to that. It may help you realize that life is truly GAIN.
- *Connecting with a sounding board:* Some of us have mentors, and those are always great to have, but remember that mentors come and go in your life. If you are fortunate enough to identify a sounding board who wants to take the time to listen and provide constructive feedback, you

will get great satisfaction from this relationship, and experience that life is really GAIN.
- *Reframing:* Reframing means that you change your mindset about something you are going through, and try to analyze it from a different angle. The point is that your first impression of something you encounter may be negative, based on your biases and the mental models you built in our mind. Reframing may be positively influenced by meditation and certain yoga practices.
- *Become a member of a contemplative circle:* There are groups for like-minded people based on practically any criterion you can think of: religion, intellectual, psychological, philosophical, practice-based, skill-based, medically-focused, and more. Finding such a group that you can become part of may be very therapeutic. These options of constructive human interaction can help you realize that life is truly GAIN.

— *The Noble Eightfold Path:* This is an ancient concept that derives from the Buddhist insight of the Four Noble truths. These are: (1) Suffering exists, (2) suffering has a cause, (3) suffering can be ended, and (4) this happens through the Noble Eightfold Path.
— *The Noble Eightfold Path* encompasses the following practices or insights: Right View; Right Intention; Right Speech; Right Action; Right Livelihood; Right Effort; Right Mindfulness; and Right Concentration.

# 9

# Leading with a GAIN Focus

**Contents**

| | |
|---|---|
| Leading with a GAIN Perspective | 114 |
| Avoid the LOSE Mindset | 121 |
| GAIN and AI | 126 |
| Chapter Highlights | 129 |

**Abstract** This chapter applies the GAIN concept in a leadership context. It considers some best practice ideas, and then alerts us about mental stances that can inhibit the practice of GAIN, some of which are, Lamenting, Obsessing, Scathing, Envying (LOSE). Each of these behaviors is reviewed in light of their disparaging effects on your advancement and overall psyche.

**The Dark Path Called Envy: A Story**

Sasha and Jenny worked together at a PR firm. Life was good and the ladies were doing well in their field. There was one major difference between them, though: Sasha would always try to learn from the advancement of others, while Jenny was plagued by a bitter sense of envy.

Even within the context of their lives—Sasha was always happy when Jenny or her loved ones accomplished something, using it as a stimulus to find out how she could improve her own life given her specific qualities. Jenny, on the other hand, had a hard time hiding her envy whenever Sasha or her family had a windfall, and this ultimately brought a rift between the two colleagues.

Sasha moved on, reinventing herself multiple times, and making some impressive professional strides along the way. Jenny made some small advancements, but never got rid of her bitterness, and continued to suffer on her dark path of envy until she retired.

---

> He is no fool who gives what he cannot keep to gain what he cannot lose.[1]
> ~Jim Elliot

## Leading with a GAIN Perspective

Regardless what leadership style you aspire, whether this would be transformational, transactional, spiritual, servant, awakened, autocratic, authentic, or a combination of some, the GAIN concept can make an important difference in the way you treat yourself and those you interact with.

First and foremost, I want you to know that leadership doesn't have to entail a position in a formal organization. I firmly believe that you can only be a good leader to others if you are a good leader to yourself. I also believe that people gravitate to the individuals they see as good self-leaders. Self-leadership is therefore a critical pathway toward a formal leadership position in case you aspire that.

In being a good self-leader, you need to be able to lead well and follow well simultaneously. You need to be able to perceive matters from a rational standpoint, and then work on your mental and emotional balance to follow the path you determined. This doesn't mean that you should not adjust when unforeseen issues arise—and they will—but as much as possible, you should keep yourself in balance. Stability works best toward your own peace of mind, and toward the peace of mind of those who surround you.

Another alert to share here is the fact that "self" is a questionable subject. We all have egos. Some bigger than we would like them to be. To keep the ego within decent proportions, it is healthy to remember Thich Nhat Hanh's notion of interbeing, and the general Buddhist psychological stance of dependent arising: everything is interconnected, and you would not be where you are today without the blood, sweat and tears of so many people and other beings you know and will never know. For that purpose alone, it may be good when you have your cereal or a sandwich in the morning to consider how

---

[1] https://www.brainyquote.com/quotes/jim_elliot_189244?src=t_gain

much effort went into getting everything you are currently having for your nourishment, the box of cereals, the milk, the raisin, the toast, the cheese, and more, in front of you. And there it is: you cannot think about the thousands, maybe millions of human and other beings that worked on making it all possible without feeling humble and grateful. That's a great mindset to start the day and place your "self" in perspective.

When you start your day, as a student, a gardener, a vice-president, a homemaker, a retire person, or in any other position, take a moment to observe yourself in the mirror, smile at the person you see, and wish them a great day. You may also put in a good wish for those you feel particularly close to, such as your children, parents, partner, pets, siblings, friends, neighbors, colleagues, you name it.

This combination of things to consider will enhance your sense of gratitude even before you face anything the outside world has in store for you. Sending good thoughts in the world is a wonderful thing to do, and if you believe in the power of thoughts, you can see how you are already contributing toward making the world a better place. The thoughts of being interconnected to everything else, and the gratitude that you are here now is a powerful way of implementing the GAIN mindset.

*Creating Educational Success Pathways for Students: Anayet Chowdhury*

Perusing Forbes' 2023 30-under-30 list, I came across a brief description of a young man who made a difference for many young people over the past 9 years. Anayet Chowdhury is the son of Bangladeshi immigrants. He cofounded ArgoPrep, an EdTech publisher specializing in K-8th grade supplemental resources. He did this in 2015 with only $60. At the time of writing this chapter, more than 1 million students and educators have used ArgoPrep materials, which include video lectures, quizzes, and printable worksheets, to boost K-8 test scores in various subjects including math, science and social studies.[2]

ArgoPrep has won many awards over the past years; a sign that its customers—students and teachers—think it works well. According to the ArgoPrep website, a high percentage of parents have confirmed that this e-learning platform is significantly helping their child improve their skills.

The surprising news about Chowdhury is that he initially set out to go to Med School, and was doing his Bachelor's in molecular biology, a passion that he has not relinquished. The MIT educational studies program describes Anayet as an author, entrepreneurial thinker, and educator who has helped thousands of students gain acceptance into top colleges and high schools. His passion is obviously geared in two directions: a love for teaching, and conducting cancer

---

[2] Anayet Chowdhury (2023). Forbes 30 under 30: Education. Retrieved from https://www.forbes.com/profile/anayet-chowdhury/?sh=3d0027f72e13

research at Memorial Sloan-Kettering Cancer Center. Mr. Chowdhury's cancer project has been awarded multiple gold-medal awards and he even had the opportunity to present his research to President Obama.[3]

On his LinkedIn webpage, Chowdhury expresses his gratitude for making it to the Forbes 30 under 30 list for 2023. He looks back at his life thus far and shares his youth experiences growing up in a 298-square-foot apartment with a family of four, living extremely frugally, because there was no money for any kind of splurging. His mom cut his hair until he was 18, because she could not afford the $10 for a haircut. The family had no cable television or high-speed internet. Yet, there was support, and there was motivation.

Chowdhury continues his story explaining how he and a group of friends, while he was doing his undergrad in molecular biology, founded Argoprep with $60, only to see it mushrooming to a gigantic project that thus far sold more than $13 million dollars in workbooks. A good part of this money has been invested in the learning platform.

Of course the path was not a bed of roses. There have been failures, and Chowdhury is sober enough to realize that there will be more of those along the way. He honestly shares that entrepreneurship is a rewarding endeavor, but not an easy one. The greatest reward lies in doing something fulfilling that also benefits others.[4]

The reason for profiling Anayet Chowdhury above is because he is a great example of conducting self-leadership through the GAIN model: he *generated* his experiences growing up in a very modest household, getting an opportunity to go to college, and falling in love with education. This *appreciation* process, which was an evaluation of what he truly liked in life, undoubtedly led to a process of *internalizing*, through which he realized that he had to do something to help young members of society succeed in attaining higher education, just like he did. The *newness* that came from this process was his entrepreneurial effort of co-founding and operating ArgoPrep: a fulfilling resource for millions of people who will become all they can be.

### Retrospect

The old up and down
Sometimes brings me a frown
Today, everything seems great

---

[3] *Anayet Chowdhury, Entrepreneur & Educator* (2023). *ESP Biography.* Retrieved from https://esp.mit.edu/teach/teachers/anayetc/bio.html
[4] *Anayet Chowdhury: CEO & Co-Founder at ArgoPrep* (2024) *LinkedIn.* Retrieved from https://www.linkedin.com/in/anayet-chowdhury-762b7195/

Tomorrow brings a twist of fate
It's an ever-swinging carrousel
That, by now, I should know well
Yet, life remains a big surprise
And maybe that's its very spice

We find ourselves moving from boom
To insecure and pitch-black doom
What keeps us hanging on this slope
Is our steady, incorrigible hope
That, even though today we whine
Tomorrow again the sun will shine
And what today may seem like night
Will transform into promising light

People come and people go
Today a friend, tomorrow foe
Positions, minds and visions change
What's normal now, was once so strange
The person that I am today
Doesn't resemble the old me in any way
So, on I bounce, between joy and sorrow
Here today, and gone tomorrow

*–Joan Marques*

## Practicing GAIN in Daily Life

Once the interactions with others start, things can get a bit more complicated. We get to deal with people and situations we may not be overly fond of. All the well-wishes in the world cannot change that. But do consider, that everything and everyone that lives, wants to be happy and be alive. Admitted, some get so desperate that they want to give it all up, but that is usually the result of tremendous stress, setbacks, rejection, and other instances of suffering.

Remember the four noble truths discussed in Chap. 8? They are always there. Suffering exists, and it has a cause, because either want something we cannot get (desire) or want to get rid of something that sticks with us (aversion).

You will encounter people who don't like you, just because you exist. No kind act from your side will make them change their mind. I wrote about that earlier in this book as well (see Chap. 3), where I encountered a woman who was reasonably nice to me until I got a job she felt I did not deserve. From then on, she ignored me in a way I considered painful, until I learned that I was making this woman's attitude more important to my performance and wellbeing than it should be.

Just like I did at that time, you also have the ability to decide our attitude. That, too, has been a statement made multiple times in this book. And it's a profound leadership strategy. You cannot prevent what happens, but you can decide how you will look at it, and what you will do about it. Sometimes it will take time to find the strength and mindset to look at a situation positively, and sometimes you may have to revert to one of the ten ways I suggested in Chap. 8, starting with meditation, and ending with membership in a contemplative circle. Better even, you can think of the Noble Eightfold Path, and practice the eight right actions and mindsets that will release negative internal tendencies and bring positive ones to the surface.

In all honesty, life is full of disruptions, and the challenges we have to face in the "generating," "Appreciating" and Internalizing" stages are sometimes so unexpected and mindboggling that we will need time to center before even beginning to perceive these challenges as part of the gains in our life. A good piece of advice: don't blame yourself, or at least, not too long (Fig. 9.1).

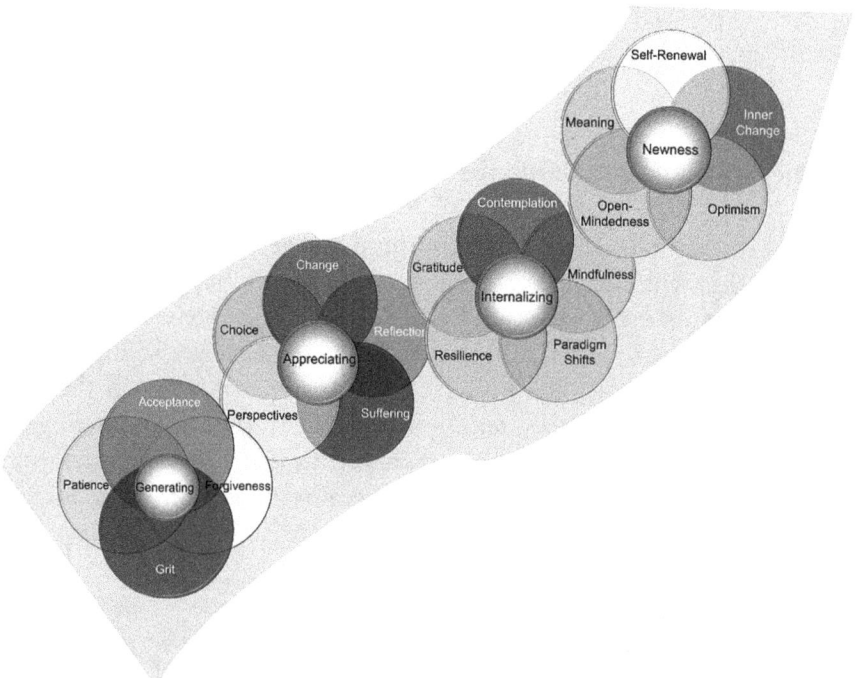

**Fig. 9.1** The GAIN Process

A while ago, I found myself in a situation that filled me with despair for some time. The place I had considered as my safe haven until retirement; where I had given my all for many years, and which I took so much pride in, was going through a transition with another entity. All of a sudden, my future was on the line. And while the rational part of my mind reasoned that changes are the only constant, that there will be a window opening for every door that closes, and that I just had to be patient to see how this would play out, the other part was engaging in self-blame and blame to others: I was kicking myself for always making the wrong decisions (why did I ever choose this place?), and others for not safeguarding the future of this place properly. All that, while there had been many good years, and while I am well aware that the current situation was a consequence of a series of factors and influences outside of our control.

I realized that this experience was yet another teacher in my life, and that there was a lesson to be learned. Maybe the lesson was that I could not control everything, and that I just needed to trust in the goodness of the universe. I decided to meditate and internalize what I had known all along: that, like my breath, everything arises and passes. This status quo that was about to change, had been in place for a long time, and needed to change, even though I, and with me many others, did not want that.

Looking back at the situation, I can only say that this event was a good, and actually past-due, "wake-up call" to prepare for newness. I realized that, while I had been complaining about the routine of my activities and the downward spiral of progress in many ways, I had refused to engage in the reinvention that had entered my mind multiple times. Based on this event, I got myself into gear, blew life into an organization I had founded but not operated over the previous four years, and took to social media to share my insights with the world. I started shifting the "challenge" into an "opportunity" by bringing together all my skills and finding the most beneficial way to merge them. The reinvention process is still ongoing, but I have now acquired a sense of gratitude for not falling prey to the sleepwalk mindset I often warn others for. Oh, how easy is it to become a sleepwalker: we nestle ourselves in a routine, and practice it day in day out, year in year out, without investing the energy to question what we should do to elevate the level of satisfaction and happiness in our life.

Thanks to this unexpected turn of events, I was basically forced to apply GAIN:

- I **generated** the experience of losing the relative comfort I had gotten accustomed to,
- I reviewed it, initially with a sense of horror, but gradually with **appreciation** for the opportunity it created,
- I **internalized** the options I had and discovered the many ways in which I could reconstruct my livelihood in a way that would grant me so much more fulfillment and happiness, and
- I am now embarking on the **newness** that I have cultivated through the process.

> **Point to Ponder**
>
> Consider a situation you are currently dealing with or have recently dealt with.
> Evaluate this situation with the elements of GAIN.
> Where do you feel there may be a bottleneck? How do you plan to overcome it?

**Mind, body, and …?**

Moving from present to future
And oftentimes also to the past
Able to imagine alternatives
To situations that didn't last
Rarely dwelling too long anywhere
Shifting, now slow, then fast
An avid traveler at its core
Here calm, but there with a blast

Like a disloyal partner it moves
Away from the body and back
In directions hard to predict
Ever flowing, alert – rarely slack
Conjuring mesmerizing thoughts
Colorful, bright, or pitch-black
Harder to pin down as you try
And not easy to keep on track

Captured in my head but not caught
The fountain of many a thought
Not even slowing down during sleep
Crossing continents in a swift leap
And if someday it stays away
This body might be led astray
And then will come the day I die
But then I wonder: who am I?

*– Joan Marques*

## Avoid the LOSE Mindset

There is an opposite to the GAIN approach, that I feel I should alert you for, as it is all too easy to fall prey to it if you don't keep your head together. Since I used an acronym to explain the fulfilling approach to life, I will also use an acronym to present the things you want to avoid. That acronym is LOSE, and here's what it stands for:

## Lamenting

While you may find yourself lamenting when you encounter a traumatic event, it is important to keep in mind that this should not become a new and lasting state of existing. We all deserve to mourn our losses, and some losses are more painful than others. But there comes a time that you have to get yourself up and move on. Don't think that moving on is unfair or shallow. I have considered that when I lost my dearest pet-friend Bella in 2019. I thought I should never get another pet, because moving on without Bella was a substandard way of living, and it was unfair to Bella, who could not be part of this life anymore.

Fortunately, I meditated on this for a while, and even though there were still tears in the years thereafter, I also learned that getting another pet, especially a rescue who did not have a fun life to start with, was a compassionate thing to do. I even realized that if Bella could communicate with me, she would let me know that I should pay the goodness forward by giving another pet a chance on a protected and cheerful lifestyle. This is how I welcomed Molly in my life, and no, she is not Bella, but she is her own precious, adorable self, who brought some light in our life again, while we were blessed to do the same for her.

Lamenting too long is not just a bad thing for your mind, it can also make you physically ill, and it will affect your relationships with others and your outlook on life. So, keep it limited, and work deliberately on converting it to a sense of gratitude about what was, and anticipation on what it to come.

In an interesting article from the Cleveland Clinic, two psychologists, Dr. Scott Bea and Dr. Susan Albers, share some great ideas on how to stop lamenting.

1. *Step back.* The issue you currently deal with is just a small part of your life. Look at it that way. It will pass.
2. *Look within.* Journal the issue that bothers you and include the reasons why you think it is such a problem in your opinion. You may obtain a deeper understanding on what is really at the root and how to address it.
3. *Make a game of it.* If you caught yourself lamenting a lot, you can adopt an exercise. Dr. Bea suggests wearing a bracelet or rubber band and change it to the other hand every time you complain. Try to keep the bracelet or rubber band on one arm for a month.
4. *Choose a proper outlet.* Don't share your concerns on social media. Keep it private and be critical in selecting your sounding board, recommends Dr. Albers.
5. *Voice sensible concerns.* Consider what you say. If you're going to complain do so by also suggesting a solution and the reason why that should be. This comes across as more mature and sensible than just uttering criticism.
6. *Identify the good parts and mention them.* Make sure your complaint begins and ends on a positive note, so that you don't leave the one(s) on the receiving end with a bad feeling.
7. *Express gratitude.* This is a recurring subject in the suggestion lists presented in this book. That makes sense, because you get so much further with expressing gratitude. If you can make gratitude the habit rather than lamenting, and if you can write between one and three reasons why you are grateful every day, the entire quality of your life will undergo a turn for the better.[5]

## Obsessing

Obsessions can sneak up on you before you know it. When you want something very much and you cannot get it, it can become an obsession. Similarly, when you want to get rid of something and you cannot, it can become an obsession. Obsessing is a dangerous state of mind, as it is irrational, and can lead to irrational acts. A friend of mine went through an ugly divorce, and after trying to mend things several times, his wife decided that it was really over. The couple had two children, which my friend was very fond of, and the fact that he could not see his children daily anymore ate at him. He started stalking his ex-wife and the children, and threatening them in the most obscene way. His mental imbalance became so bad that he ultimately did some major damage to the home of his ex-wife and kids, leading him to be arrested and jailed for three months. Three long months, in which he lost his job, and one of his precious dogs, since he now had to count on others to look after everything.

---

[5] Cleveland Clinic (29 Aug 2018). How to Stop Complaining: 7 Secrets to Being Happier. *Health Essentials.* Retrieved from https://health.clevelandclinic.org/how-to-stop-complaining-7-secrets-to-being-happier

It took my friend a long time to overcome his obsession. His ex-wife had to get a restraining order, which did not make things more bearable. Over the course of the next three years, he finally calmed down, and the former couple developed a reasonable, mature communication bond, with mutual respect and clear boundaries on both sides.

Obsessing happens, and it is never good, as it robs you from your rational senses, and can transform you into a pitiful being, feared by others, and not very likeable, least of all to yourself. If, therefore, you feel as if you are obsessing over something, seek help. Talk to a mentor or a therapist, or, if you can muster the strength, meditate in order to gain the insight that you are not doing yourself a favor with this attitude.

In a brief article in Psychology Today, Dr. Seth Meyers suggests a few simple steps to disrupt obsessive thoughts and help guide your mind in a different direction. He recommends starting by acknowledging that you are upset about something. Then, ask yourself the following questions:

- If I had to guess, what is the exact temperature now here?
- What is my body temperature like now? Do I feel a little cold, a little warm, or perfectly comfortable?
- If I don't make any noise, can I identify every single sound that I hear?
- Outside, what is in the sky? Are there clouds? How would I describe what I see in the sky?
- On a scale of 1 to 10, how hungry am I?
- If I could choose to eat any dish right, what would I choose?

The exercise above serves as a distraction to your mind from the upsetting thoughts in which you were stuck. Dr. Meyers alerts us that the above questions could be expanded or replaced by other simple, neutralizing questions, as long as they level your mindset and distract you from the upsetting thoughts.[6]

## Scathing

Some people have the pitiful habit to engage in scathing when things don't turn out the way they had hoped. Scathing is mean. It negatively affects your mind, and it alienates others from you. Unfortunately, some people have made scathing their second nature. They seem to be in the habit of deriding others, and I suspect that they do that in a desperate effort to make them feel better about themselves. You may have heard the saying, "Misery loves

---

[6] Meyers, S. (Dec. 82,016). Stop Obsessing or Fixating With a Fast Cognitive Technique. *Psychology Today*. Retrieved from https://www.psychologytoday.com/us/blog/insight-is-2020/201612/stop-obsessing-or-fixating-fast-cognitive-technique

company"? People who mock others are most likely miserable. They have a deep-rooted unhappiness inside that they can only temporarily silence by making others miserable as well.

I knew a man who would always point out anything that was less perfect in others. He was making deriding comments to his overweight daughter, mocked his wife regularly about the way she dressed, insulted his son in front of his friends at every opportunity he had, and thought he was funny when he made fun of others. Unfortunately, this man never changed, even though he is a senior citizen today. Life handed him several warning signs, and every time it seemed as if he would change for the better, only to fall into the same scathing pattern as soon as he recovered. The sad part of the story is that this man was probably miserable inside, and with that, he left no chance unused to make others miserable as well. Don't be like this person.

> If you are the one who engages in making scathing remarks to others whenever you feel displeased, or if you engage in any other bad habit, try the following set of actions to keep yourself in control:

1. *Make It Conscious*: Figure out why you do what you do. If you can find out when you do it, you are getting close to the reason, and you may succeed in putting a stop to the act.
2. *Write it down*: Describe your act, but also what caused it, how you felt, and what went through your head. If you feel that your habit brings you some satisfaction, write that down as well. If you do this for one or two weeks, then read back, you may be able to see a pattern and decide on a behavioral change to end the bad habit.
3. *Bait and Switch*: Once you have discovered the foundational reasons behind your bad habit, find a less-damaging substitute for it. If you feel like insulting someone, you could take a piece of gum to chew on instead, or whistle a tune that calms you down. You can also focus on your breathing: do walking or sitting meditation to remind yourself about the arising and passing of everything, and allow your tendency to say something hurtful to pass.[7]

If, conversely, you are the one being the subject of your partner's, parent's, child's or colleague's scathing remarks, consider the following:

- *Calm yourself down before responding.* You don't need a scathing contest or something worse. Calmly consider the possible reasons behind the scathing party's comments. If you figure out that it may be jealousy, a sense of inferiority, or just general anger, you can start feeling compassion and send forgiving thoughts to this poor culprit.

---

[7] Mann, D. (Nov. 162007). 3 Easy Steps to Breaking Bad Habits. *WebMD*. Retrieved from https://www.webmd.com/balance/features/3-easy-steps-to-breaking-bad-habits

- *Consider the validity of the criticism.* There may be a core of useful truth in even the worst insult. So, step over your sense of hurt and take a hard look at the facts, and any possible grounds for improvement that you could learn from and work on.
- *Thank the person who offered the criticism.* Sometimes what we experience as scathing may be a well-intended effort to help you improve. And regardless whether the comments were meant to be hurtful or not, thanking the other party may make them rethink their negativity.
- *Carry on.* Once you have responded gracefully and evaluated the message on its merit for your wellbeing and progress, you can decide what to do with the message. Just don't allow it to stop you from doing great things. That's what you are here to do anyway.[8]

## Envying

One of the worst things you can do to yourself is to envy others. First of all, you most likely don't know the entire story of how they got where they are, and even if you do, envy is never the way to grow. When someone accomplishes something, it is much better to turn inward and use this as a motivator to improve yourself as well. This is how we can make the world a better place: by converting our observations into motivations for improvement rather than bitterness.

We all get multiple chances in our life, and it's up to us to seize the opportunities. Unfortunately, it's the people who forego their own chances when they appear, that envy others most. This is a serious flaw, but it is one that you can overcome if you find that you have been troubled by it. If you see others doing well, turn inward and ask yourself what you need to do to improve your own life. Most of the time you already know the answer. The art is to follow up on your own advise. It's not easy. It usually takes hard work, perseverance, grit... but you can do it.

A good summary of actions to overcome envy is suggested below, inspired by The Book of Joy by the Dalai Lama, Desmond Tutu, and Douglas Abrams:

- *Envy only hurts the envious.* If you want to be a happy person, you should stop envying others, even if it seems that they are more successful than you. Comparing is a bad habit anyway, especially when it leads to feelings of distress rather than the will to just do better on your own merit.
- *Gratitude.* When you feel a sense of envy emerging, replace it with gratitude. Think of all you have accomplished and the things that are going well in your life. There is always reason and space for thankfulness.

---

[8] Babauta, L. (ND). The Art of Handling Criticism Gracefully. *Zen Habits*. Retrieved from https://zenhabits.net/criticism/

- *Transform Envy into Motivation.* Just like with the introductory story to this chapter, you can convert envy into motivation to do your best in the areas where you are gifted. Your ability to shine may lay in a different field, but that doesn't mean that it's any less.
- *Reframe Your Envy.* It's not all god that glitters. Every accomplishment comes with some challenges. Consider that when overcome by envy: you may not even truly want what the other party has if you consider all that goes with it. So, be sober about it, and keep yourself in balance.
- *Apply Mudita.* The Dalai Lama suggests adding some 'mudita' to your life. Mudita is a Tibetan way of being happy for others when they succeed. It can be seen in light of our interbeing: if we are all interconnected, then the blessings of others are also partly ours. This mindset will encourage us to wish the other party well, and rejoice in their fortune.
- *Let Go and Relax.* That is the best favor you can do yourself, health wise. Envy brings stress, and there are so many people who are very successful and never have enough. They constantly envy others. Don't be that way. It's poisonous to your health and wellness. So, let go and relax.[9]

> **Point to Ponder**
>
> Which of the four elements of LOSE have you detected in yourself? How have you dealt with it, and if not yet, how will you from here onward? Which of the four LOSE behaviors do you consider most destructive? To whom and why?

## GAIN and AI

So far, Artificial Intelligence (AI) has not been a factor of discussion in this book, because the content is very much focused on human awareness toward more fulfilled and rewarded living. I believe, however, that given the importance of AI in today's world, some observations should be in place.

AI is the collective reference to a machine's ability to execute intellectual functions that we associate with human minds, such as perceiving, reasoning, learning, interacting with the environment, problem-solving, decision-making, and even demonstrating creativity.[10] There have been major outbursts

---

[9] Bokhari, D. (ND). Overcoming Envy. *Meaningful HQ*. Retrieved from https://www.meaningfulhq.com/overcoming-envy.html

[10] Rai, A., Constantinides, P., & Sarker, S. (2019). Next-generation digital platforms: Toward human–AI hybrids. *MIS Quarterly, 43*(1), iii–ix.

of enthusiasm and excitement, especially amongst scientists, about the accelerated emergence of AI in recent years. Similarly, there has been immense apprehension amongst current and future members of the workforce regarding the potential of AI taking over their jobs and making the human factor insignificant in various professional actions.

With investments in AI predicted to reach $232 billion by 2025, and with an ever-expanding use of AI in industries varying from marketing and healthcare to finance, including ever broadening interactions with internal and external human stakeholders, it becomes important to start thinking about the responsibility that will have to be taken—and by whom—when AI practices turn out to be unethical or harmful. Depending on the severity of the damage, it has thus far been that the machine developers are mostly held accountable, followed by the companies offering the AI service, and AI itself.[11]

Questions have also been raised by scholars and various actors in society, whether AI could be assigned a decision-making position in any interactional setting, for instance, in democratic participation. The very fact that this question is raised today has offended many individuals, who feel that democratic participation has always been the privilege of human beings, and AI is not human. Additionally, receiving its communicative and reasoning abilities from algorithms, it is hard to imagine a situation where this systemic construction should be allowed to participate in political decision-making on equal terms with humans.[12] The skepticism in granting AI a place in the decision-making ranks of major entities is largely based on the claim that AI lacks the relevant cognitive faculties, primarily intuition, which is often needed at those levels.[13]

However, there are strong expectations that de development of intelligence levels for AI will increase in future decades to the point that it will match human intelligence. Since AI has seen a strong development in healthcare, the question on the table is therefore, whether AI scientists should be subject to the Hippocratic Oath.[14]

---

[11] Sullivan, Y. W., & Fosso Wamba, S. (2022). Moral judgments in the age of artificial intelligence. *Journal of Business Ethics, 178*(4), 917–943.

[12] Beckman, L., & Rosenberg, J. H. (2022). The democratic inclusion of artificial intelligence? exploring the patiency, agency and relational conditions for demos membership. *Philosophy & Technology, 35*(2).

[13] Khan, A., Jillani, M.A.H.S. and Maseehullah, M. (2019). Killer Robots and Their Compliance with the Principles of Law of War. *Available at SSRN*: https://ssrn.com/abstract=3840427

[14] Siafakas, N. M. (2021). Do we need a hippocratic oath for artificial intelligence scientists? *AI Magazine, 42*(4), 57–61.

All of the above ruminations serve as a contemplative point to all of us regarding the role of AI in our daily life, and its prominence in our current and future undertakings. As AI develops in the future, awareness-based practices may have to be reviewed on their applicability to non-human colleagues and society members. However, as matters currently stand, the GAIN concept would not be applicable to AI. One could make the point that AI does engage in *generating, appreciating, internalizing,* and renewing (*newness*), but the *conscious* foundation that is needed to interpret experiences, evaluate how they made us feel, and considering them within the wholeness of a lifetime toward ongoing newness, with attention to moral righteousness, personal and societal wellness, and resilience, is thus far a human prerogative, that cannot be implemented through algorithms. Thus far, researchers are generally in agreement that it will be challenging for a machine to achieve advanced stages of consciousness, in particular reflective consciousness, which demands multi-levels of cognitive abilities such as awareness of awareness, thinking about thinking, or knowledge of knowledge, along with the will to make choices and act on them.[15]

**The Leader Inside**

This path I am treading
Is paved by the choices I made
And will evolve as a result
Of how through life I wade

While the world outside
May influence the tide
My perspectives and actions
Make my path narrow or wide

I may not be in charge
Of whatever might emerge
But my attitude guides me
In converting drought to surge

The leader of my life
I am, without a doubt
I'm grateful for my steps
In living good, gentle, yet stout

*-Joan Marques*

---

[15] Meissner, G. (2020). Artificial intelligence: Consciousness and conscience. *AI & Society, 35*(1), 225–235.

## Chapter Highlights

- *Leading with a GAIN Perspective:* This can make an important difference in the way you treat yourself and those you interact with.
- *Being a good self-leader:* this means that you need to be able to lead well and follow well simultaneously. Stability works best toward your own peace of mind, and toward the peace of mind of those who surround you.
- *"Self" is a questionable subject.* We all have egos. To keep the ego within decent proportions, it is healthy to remember Thich Nhat Han's notion of interbeing, and the general Buddhist psychological stance of dependent arising.
- *Interactions with people can be ambivalent.* We get to deal with people and situations we may not be overly fond of. But do consider, that everything and everyone that lives, wants to be happy and be alive.
- *You have the ability to decide our attitude.* You cannot prevent what happens, but you can decide how you will look at it, and what you will do about it.
- *Avoid the LOSE Mindset.* LOSE stands for:

  - *Lamenting:* We all deserve to mourn our losses, and some losses are more painful than others. But there comes a time that you have to get yourself up and move on. Lamenting too long is not just a bad thing for your mind, it can also make you physically ill, and it will affect your relationships with others and your outlook on life.
  - *Obsessing:* When you want something very much and you cannot get it, it can become an obsession. Similarly, when you want to get rid of something and you cannot, it can become an obsession. Obsessing is a dangerous state of mind, as it is irrational, and can lead to irrational acts. If, therefore, you feel as if you are obsessing over something, seek help.
  - *Scathing:* Scathing is mean. It negatively affects your mind, and it alienates others from you. Unfortunately, some people have made scathing their second nature. They seem to be in the habit of deriding others, and it's very likely that they do that in a desperate effort to make them feel better about themselves. People who mock others are most likely miserable. They have a deep-rooted unhappiness inside that they can only temporarily silence by making others miserable as well.
  - *Envying:* One of the worst things you can do to yourself is to envy others. When someone accomplishes something, it is much better to turn inward and use this as a motivator to improve yourself as well. This is how we can make the world a better place: by converting our observations into motivations for improvement rather than bitterness.

# 10

# A Mindful Journey

**Contents**

| | |
|---|---|
| Mental Models: The Good and Bad | 133 |
| Mental Models and Mindfulness | 134 |
| Balancing Left and Right Brain | 137 |
| Practicing Leadershift | 138 |
| Keeping the Journey GAINful | 140 |
| Chapter Highlights | 142 |

**Abstract** This final chapter reemphasizes the importance of remaining mindful of your mental models, as you can easily slide into negative thought patterns, influenced by circumstances, practices, or people who surround you. We will look into the importance of mindfulness for our mental models, sharing a piece of advice on leadershifting, and explain the acronym COURAGE in light of the GAIN model.

**The Impact of Altruism: A Story**

Jim had been a high performing loner for most of his life. The people he worked with admired his work, and one day the company president asked Jim to take on the position of manager in the production department.

Jim reluctantly accepted, as he was aware that he would now have to shift his behavior from doing everything for his own progress to motivating and pulling along an entire department.

Because Jim did not like losing, he made sure his department excelled. He did everything he could to catapult even the weakest co-worker ahead, much to the pleasure of upper administration.

As Jim neared retirement, he requested a return to a less responsible position, and now it was the president's turn to reluctantly agree. During his last years on the job, Jim was allowed to re-engage in his self-uplifting performance, but something had changed: Jim found out that shifting to an altruistic approach during his management years had rubbed off positively on his psyche, and he kept assisting others toward betterment till the end.

> With mindfulness, you can establish yourself in the present in order to touch the wonders of life that are available in that moment.[1]
>
> ~Thich Nhat Hanh

**Confronting our Biases**

Where is the truth? That virtuous friend:
Impartial reality without a smudge?
It lives outside our biased mind
And is, regrettably, hard to find
In the mental rubble through which we judge

Our biases are alive and well
Fueling our views and emotions
Culture, religion, family and peers
They instilled in us the joys and fears
That now influence many of our notions

Being aware of this human shortfall
Is dreadful, but also enlightening
As it motivates our brains
To transcend their constraints
And embrace what once seemed frightening

It's been too long now, that we indulged
In thoughts of inferior versus supreme
Judging on accents, sex, skin-colors
Age, skills, or assumed wealth in dollars
It's time to release that obsolete dream

---

[1] https://www.brainyquote.com/quotes/thich_nhat_hanh_591335

Becoming mindful of our biases
Is liberating and drives spiritual rebirth
None of us stands beneath or above
The ability to embrace and love
All that lives with us on Mother Earth

*-Joan Marques*

## Mental Models: The Good and Bad

We all have mental models. They are the shortcuts our mind has created to make quick decisions, based on past impressions. Mental models can come out handy in multiple settings, such as when you need to select a product or service or when you need to practice a concept. Mental models are the foundations to how you see the world and react to the things that happen around you.[2] And because they are shortcuts based on past impressions, you can surmise that mental models should be assessed and updated at times, but truth is that we rarely do so. The main reason for that is that we're often not even aware that we have mental models. We build them instinctively and stick to them from there on. It's only when someone points them out, like on this page, that you may start realizing how dependent your daily practices, actions, and reactions are on your mental models.

The good part of mental models is that they accelerate your decision-making processes. It would be rather time consuming if you'd have to engage in deep contemplation every time you needed to make a quick decision on a recurring matter at work, in the supermarket, or in your interactions with friends. And, admitted, some mental models don't need revising, because they don't harm your progress or influence the wellbeing of others.

The bad part of mental models is that some of them do influence our perceptions. This is when they become implicit biases.[3] In those cases, your mental models can affect the selections you make in hiring people, and if you're not open to diversity, for instance, a mental model can limit your selection of co-workers to people who look, walk, talk, and think just like you. As you can gather, that is not a good development in work environments where the intention is to be creative and innovative. A homogeneous team tends to think along the same lines, which may on one hand be time efficient, but on the other hand negatively affects out of the box thinking and acting.

---

[2] Clear, J. (2018). Mental Models: Learn How to Think Better and Gain a Mental Edge. *JamesClear.com*. Retrieved from https://jamesclear.com/mental-models#:~:text=The%20phrase%20%E2%80%9C mental%20model%E2%80%9D%20is,understand%20how%20the%20economy%20works
[3] Clark, B. G., & Underwood, O. D. (2019). Mitigating implicit bias as a leader. *JOM*, 71(7), 2152–2155.

Human beings are interesting in many ways, and one of them is that we gravitate toward people that resemble us in the ways that matter to us. These ways could be but are not limited to looks, habits, culture, education, religious conviction, generation, ethnicity, gender, or any other orientation. So, mental models are not perfect, even though we use them all the time.

Now that you are aware of the fact that you operate with mental models, you can start examining them on a regular basis, and adjust them by implementing structures to minimize their damaging effects, for instance, by enriching your decision-making team with diverse members or by removing personal details from documents if you need to evaluate applicants.

## Mental Models and Mindfulness

There is a clear link between successfully applying your mental models and practicing mindfulness. By being mindful, you maintain awareness of the need that things change, and that you should respect the evolving nature of everything, including your perspectives on things and people, your work environments, and the way things are done today.

There is so much changing around us all the time. I have heard even young people expressing their amazement about the pace in which new social media channels, opportunities and trends emerge, and how quickly old patterns get obsolete. Imagine what it must be like for the older ones among us!

Throughout this morass of evolutions, we must nurture our mindfulness, otherwise we can get lost, and fall prey to mindlessly following trends and patterns that are not in tune with our current focus or purpose. The practical suggestions I offered in Chap. 8, such as meditating, yoga, taking long walks, journaling, and more, are also great avenues to keep your mindfulness intact.

Engaging in mindfulness practices increases your mental flexibility and self-awareness, while it will also enable you to be a better leader when situations are complicated.[4] Mindfulness practices are of high value in leading organizations and can cultivate three meta competencies: (1) Metacognition, which helps you to retain calmness to oversee situations in ambiguous situations, thus make more rational decisions; (2) Acceptance, which enables you to see things as they are, and not tainted by judgmental notions, and (3) Curiosity, which is the healthy input to infuse our awareness in the moment and stay alert.[5]

---

[4] Chacksfield, E. (2017). DEVELOPING A RESILIENT MINDSET. *Training Journal*, 23–26.
[5] Reiz and Chalkson (2016). How to Bring Mindfulness to Your Company. *Harvard Business Review*.

> **Point to Ponder**
>
> Reflect on some of your mental models.
> List some that you consider helpful in your day-to-day life. How are they helpful?
> List at least one that you are not so proud of. How do you plan to work on correcting this mental model?

## Making a Difference by Practicing Mindfulness: Chade-Meng Tan

Chade-Meng Tan may have held the most unique job-title when he worked as employee no. 107 at Google: *"Jolly Good Fellow (Which Nobody Can Deny)."* Tan started as an engineer at Google, and eventually shifted from Engineering to People Operations. His job description was, "Enlighten minds, open hearts, create world peace".[6] In this position, Tan developed mindfulness training courses based on the notion that happiness is a state of mind. The training courses were meant to help his fellow Googlers find inner peace and clear their minds to manage stress and negativity. He wrote a best-selling book in 2014, *Search Inside Yourself*, named after his groundbreaking mindfulness-based emotional intelligence course at Google with the same title.

As a Googler, Tan traveled the world to speak about mindfulness at conferences and seminars. He retired from Google at age 45, as he decided to enlarge his horizons and work more actively toward his goal of helping establish world peace. During the past decade, Tan wrote two more books, *"Joy on Demand"* (2017), and *"Buddhism for All"* (2023).

On his website, Tan describes himself as an award-winning engineer, a two times New York Times bestselling author, a movie producer, and a philanthropist whose work has received eight nominations for the Nobel Peace Prize.

Reading about this man is refreshing because you find out that he has a great sense of humor. One of his statements on his website accompanying him in lotus position is: "Joy is when you're in deep sit." Tan's sense of humor radiates throughout his website. He created a bio page in line with the requirements of the modern western world. He has a tiny two-sentence version, a 200+ words version, and a full version.

---

[6] Bio. (29 March 2021). *Chade Meng.* Retrieved from https://chademeng.com/about/bio/

Among his many rewarding activities, Tan delivered a TED talk on compassion at the United Nations and spoke at the White House about the development of kindness. He has a wall filled with pictures he took with prominent people, including presidents, business moguls, celebrities, and even the Dalai Lama. His personal motto is, "Life is too important to be taken seriously".[7]

Aside from all the uplifting experiences, Tan's story reveals that in everyone's life there are dark moments that can cause a person to seriously questions themselves. In 2018 he had to step down from his position as chair of the *Search Inside Yourself Leadership Institute* (SIYLI), which promotes mindfulness and emotional intelligence. He did so at the board's request after a third-party investigation into an unspecified behavior in the past, that was referred to as "inappropriate behavior".[8] Upon stepping down, Tan expressed his regret for having contributed to the suffering of others in the past, and commented that he would deeply reflect on that, but no further explanations were given, neither by Tan, not by members of the organization from which he stepped down.

In more recent days, Tan seems to have regained his sparkling, humorous way. Perhaps he never lost it. He continues to speak on global forums, and his most recent book was received well.

Among Tan's wise pieces of advice is a 5-minute self-leadership exercise, which he recommends to everyone. He states,

> *Whenever I have a fight with my wife or a co-worker, I go to another room to calm down and after a few minutes of calming down, I do this exercise: I visualize the other person in the next room and remind myself that this person is just like me, wants to be free from suffering just like me, wants to be happy just like me, and so on. And then I wish that person wellness, happiness, and freedom from suffering.*
>
> *After just a few minutes of doing this, I feel much better about myself, about the other person, and about the whole situation. A large part of my anger dissipates immediately.*[9]

---

[7] Profile: Chade-Meng Tan (2024). Greater Good Magazine. Retrieved from https://greatergood.berkeley.edu/profile/chade_meng_tan

[8] Eaton, J. (August 21 2018). Google's former mindfulness guru steps down from nonprofit over 'inappropriate behavior'. *Think Progress*. Retrieved from https://archive.thinkprogress.org/googles-former-mindfulness-guru-steps-down-from-nonprofit-over-inappropriate-behavior-2e7bb2a8e6c3/

[9] Lebowitz, S. and Shibu, S. (Nov 26, 2019). A former Google engineer uses a 5-minute practice to defuse conflicts at home and at work. Here's how to use it at the Thanksgiving table. *Business Insider*. Retrieved from https://www.businessinsider.com/chade-meng-tan-how-to-practice-loving-kindness-2017-6

> **Point to Ponder**
>
> Read or listen to some more information about Chade-Meng Tan. What positive message can you take away from this person's story? Any words of caution you would like to share about Tan's story?

## Balancing Left and Right Brain

One of the fortunate developments about living in today's day and age is that we witness a positive trend in enhanced awareness among society members from various walks of life. While our entire education system is still very much focused on developing our left-brain hemisphere, we now discover that there is gradually some more acknowledgment for our right-brain hemisphere. Our right hemisphere is the one that processes our thoughts in a holistic way, while the left hemisphere works more in a logical and methodical manner. You could compare these two hemispheres with two sets of computer hardware that use completely different operating systems.[10]

In the past decades we have witnessed and collectively endured some mind-boggling challenges, not limited to the great recession, a wide range of various social justice-based movements, climate hazards and health scares. All these challenges may have felt as bad developments at first, but over time we have also learned to see their benefits for our collective advancement. This is mindfulness in action. And we know by now that the advantages and advancements of mindfulness are extensive.

When we work with others, we may consider ways to help elevate our right-brain hemisphere with some nice exercise that most people enjoy. Some of these are:

- Guided meditation: A popular topic in this book, indeed. But there is a reason for that. Meditation is increasingly becoming a known practice in universities and workplaces throughout the world. And the practice can be kept short enough to avoid restlessness amongst the participants.[11]

---

[10] Alder, H. (1994). The technology of creativity. *Management Decision, 32*(4), 23–29.
[11] Marques, J. F., Dhiman, S., Holt, S., & Wood, A. (2023). Activating the right hemisphere in business minds. *Development and Learning in Organizations, 37*(5), 5–7

- Poetry: During a work retreat or on a Friday afternoon, it might be nice to spend an hour or so on poetry. You could attach poems from various poets and on various topics on the wall and inviting participants to first walk around and read them. After that, you invite them to go pick their favorite poem from the wall, read it out loud and reflect. You will find that this practice of sharing favorite poems creates a sense of connection and camaraderie.[12]
- Lollipop moments: This is inspired by Drew Dudley's TEDx Talk,[13] "Everyday Leadership," in which he explains the phenomenon "Lollipop Moments" as sharing constructive comments that positively impact the lives of others. You can do a lollipop moment round by inviting members from your team to observe one another and write a positive note from the heart about each other. As the moderator, you can then collect all comments about each colleague and hand them those to take with them. Some people get so touched by the kind things colleagues write that they keep these notes forever.[14]

> **Point to Ponder**
>
> Do you consider yourself more a left brain or more a right brain person? Why?
> How is your left-brain hemisphere useful in your daily practices?
> How is your right-brain hemisphere useful in your daily practices?

## Practicing Leadershift

If you perform in a leadership position, you will have found out that today's workplaces are more complex than ever before. We see greater diversity and higher levels of collective intelligence amongst our internal and external stakeholders, and stress levels are high causing the levels of internal and external change to require more insight and flexibility than before. You will find that there is a challenge tied to every positive development. To give a few examples, (1) diversity in a team prompts expanded design thinking, fairness, and

---

[12] Ibid.
[13] Dudley, D. (2010). Everyday leadership. *TEDx-Toronto, 2010*. Available at: www.ted.com/talks/drew_dudley_everyday_leadership
[14] Marques, J. F., Dhiman, S., Holt, S., & Wood, A. (2023). Activating the right hemisphere in business minds. *Development and Learning in Organizations, 37*(5), 5–7.

stakeholder support, but it also necessitates greater conflict resolution skills and sensitivity to a wider range of cultural and traditional customs[15]; (2) increased collective intelligence within a team raises general insight, environmental awareness, and dealing with complexities,[16] but it also requires more tolerance for being questioned and criticized about decisions; and (3) accelerated change reduces monotonous routines and organizational myopia and increases performance excellence, but it can be an energy drain and pose a threat to your leadership skills and values, which can lead to potential change fatigue and change resistance.[17]

Even though the above examples represent some important challenges you will have to deal with in leading others, they are primarily of an external nature. Your biggest challenge remains the internal one. Here's the challenge in a nutshell: when you strive for a leadership position, you do so with ambition as your foundational mindset; you consider yourself a visionary, and are led by your ego, which may have served you well till that point, because it enabled you to shift ahead when others gave up. Your ego was fueled by some admirable traits such as resilience, courage, perseverance, and confidence. These, and a number of other inborn qualities helped you make swift decisions and plow your way ahead.

Yet, once you have made it to the leadership ranks, there is a critical shift many people overlook, and that is the leadershift. What this means, is that you will now have to change your driving motives from self-focused to team-focused. This shift from "me" to "we" can be difficult, especially if you have always lived and worked in an individually driven society.

Understanding the balance between the qualities that get you in the saddle and the ones that will make you do well is a critical piece of awareness in today's leadership. Once you have stepped into a leadership position, your mindset will need to move toward increased altruism, which means that you will have to place others' objectives before our own.[18] Engaging in altruism means that you will care for the wellbeing and progress of your stakeholders

---

[15] Marques. J. (2008). Workplace diversity: Developing a win-win-win strategy. *Development and Learning in Organizations. 22*(5), 5–8.

[16] Bonabeau. E. (2009). Decisions 2.0: The power of collective intelligence. *MIT Sloan Management Review. 50*(2), 45–52.

[17] McMillan. K. & Perron. A. (2020). Ideological tensions amidst rapid and continuous organizational change in healthcare. *Journal of Organizational Change Management. 33*(6), 1029–1039.

[18] Singh. N. & Krishnan. V. R. (2008). Self-sacrifice and transformational leadership: Mediating role of altruism. *Leadership & Organization Development Journal. 29*(3), 261–274.

without any benefits or accolades to you.[19] Your sense of altruism becomes critical when the overall quality of your team is being assessed, and you, the leader, realize that your team is only as strong as its weakest link. Since replacing the weakest link is not as easy as it may sound, and not as morally responsible either, your best bet is to elevate the strength of your weakest link. That is not an easy feat either, but it is an admirable one.

The need for a leader to shift from ego-driven to altruistic behavior makes more sense in today's world than it has ever made before. Contemporary workers, while still in need of their monthly paycheck, seek—above anything else—intrinsic motivation in their work. They want to feel that what they do matters in the process of performing toward a common goal, and that they, too, improve through the progression of their labor.

So, with the above explained, it may be clear that you, as a leader, will have to ensure a proper balance in your mental and emotional approach toward leading others and your workplace toward ongoing growth. Yes, your qualities of resilience, courage, confidence, and perseverance will remain, but the aggressive edges of individualism will need to make place for a more collectivist mindset, wherein you, as the leader, will increasingly find yourself engaging in acts that benefit their followers rather than yourself.

> **Point to Ponder**
>
> Do you believe altruism is appropriate in work environments? Why or why not?
> Which personal qualities have thus far been most beneficial for your progress in life?
> Which qualities do you feel you need to work on? How do you plan to do that?

## Keeping the Journey GAINful

Here are some final thoughts to help ensure your optimal benefit from the GAIN mindset in your life. Several of these thoughts have been presented throughout the book but placing them in this overview may serve as a reminder of their value and essence to your wellbeing and progress. I have also placed these essentials in an acronym, called COURAGE.

---

[19] Rohman. F. Noermijati. N.. Soelton. M. & MugioM. (2022). Model altruism in improving organizational performance in social welfare institutions ministry of social affairs of the republic of Indonesia. *Cogent Business & Management.* 9(1), 1–13.

- **C**hoice
  When things are becoming problematic, don't think you have no choices. Life always offers you choices. You may not like the options, but there are choices, and it will be up to you to think innovatively and define some choices others may not have considered. This points at the entrepreneurial spirit we all have when push comes to shove. It can help to grab a pencil and a piece of paper and write down all choice-options you can come up with in an ongoing situation, no matter how ridiculous they may sound. You may be on to discovering a gem.
- **O**pen-mindedness
  Keep your eyes and your mind wide open. Be cautious about the boundaries that you unwillingly erected, which can inhibit your progress in life. I mentioned these examples in Chap. 1: (1) Sleepwalking, which is the process of mindlessly following your routine without questioning what, how, and why you do what you do; (2) Comfort Zone Clinging, which is what we do when allow our insecurities and fears for the future stand in the way of our progress, and (3) Implicit Biases (the "bad part of mental models), which lead us to judge others based on a process of stereotyping, thus depriving ourselves and those around us from optimal progress.
- **U**sefulness
  Nothing is wasted: a foundational perspective presented in this book. If you hear someone tell you that their visit somewhere, the class they took, the job they did, or the event they attended was a waste of time, you should realize how blind-sighted this person is. Nothing is wasted. Everything serves a purpose, even if you cannot connect the dots right away. This concept was presented in Chap. 4. I mentioned there that there is a good use for every experience in your life, even though it may take some time before the pieces of the puzzle fall together.
- **R**eality-Check
  This is a call for making sure that your mental models are not limiting your progress, and that your reality remains void of limiting patterns. It also hints to the fact that no two realities are the same: each of us have our own way of looking at the world, influenced by our unique individual history and experience processing. If you realize this, you will respect other people's viewpoints better, even if those deviate from yours.
- **A**ttitude
  In several chapters of this book, starting in Chap. 5, I mentioned Epictetus and Victor Frankl, who, even though they lived many centuries apart, shared the same valuable advice to their audience: everything can be taken away from you but your attitude. You decide how you look at the things

that emerge in your life, and then determine your response. Keep a positive mindset.
- **Genius**
There is a genius in each of us. The unfortunate truth is that we have been slapped a few times too often on our hands to "draw between the lines", with which I mean to say: don't dare to be original but follow the rules. Our society has become so rule-bound, that many of us have forgotten our unique insights and practices. Our inner genius may be subdued, but is still alive., It's up to us if we want to revive it or not.
- **Education**
Keep on learning. You don't have to embark on a long educational journey if that's not your cup of tea, but keep on learning through the many avenues that we have at our disposal today: mass media, colleagues, friends, mentors, books, and our own previous mind.

Yes, it takes courage to see life as GAIN, but once you do, you'll feel more fulfilled, content, and happy.

## Chapter Highlights

- *Mental Models:* We all have mental models. They are the shortcuts our mind has created to make quick decisions, based on past impressions. Mental models are the foundations to how you see the world and react to the things that happen around you.

  - The good part of mental models is that they accelerate your decision-making processes.
  - The bad part of mental models is that some of them do influence your perceptions of people. This is when they become implicit biases.

- *Mental Models and Mindfulness:* By being mindful, you maintain awareness of the need that things change, and that you should respect the evolving nature of everything, including your perspectives on things and people, your work environments, and the way things are done today. Engaging in mindfulness practices increases your mental flexibility and self-awareness, while it will also enable you to be a better leader when situations are complicated.
- *Balancing Left and Right Brain:* Our right hemisphere processes our thoughts in a holistic way, while the left hemisphere works more in a logi-

cal and methodical manner. When we work with others, we may consider ways to help elevate our right-brain hemisphere with some nice exercise that most people enjoy. Some of these are:

- Guided meditation
- Poetry
- Lollipop moments

— *Practicing Leadershift:* Understanding the balance between the qualities that get you in the leadership saddle and the ones that will make you do well while practicing leadership is a critical piece of awareness in today's leadership. Once you have stepped into a leadership position, your mindset will need to move toward increased altruism, which means that you will have to place others' objectives before our own. The need for a leader to shift from ego-driven to altruistic behavior makes more sense in today's world than it has ever made before.
— *Keeping the Journey GAINful:* Here are some final thoughts to help ensure your optimal benefit from the GAIN mindset in your life. I have also placed these essentials in an acronym, called COURAGE.

- *Choice:* Life always offers you choices. You may not like the options, but there are choices, and it will be up to you to think innovatively and define some choices others may not have considered.
- *Open-mindedness:* Keep your eyes and your mind wide open. Be cautious about the boundaries that you unwillingly erected, which can inhibit your progress in life.
- *Usefulness:* Nothing is wasted. Everything serves a purpose, even if you cannot connect the dots right away.
- *Reality-Check:* Make sure that your mental models are not limiting your progress, and that your reality remains void of limiting patterns.
- *Attitude*: Everything can be taken away from you but your attitude. You decide how you look at the things that emerge in your life, and then determine your response. Keep a positive mindset.
- *Genius:* There is a genius in each of us. Unfortunately, our society has become so rule-bound, that many of us have forgotten our unique insights and practices. Our inner genius may be subdued, but is still alive., It's up to us if we want to revive it or not.
- *Education:* Keep on learning through the many avenues that you have at your disposal: mass media, colleagues, friends, mentors, books, and your own previous mind.

### Happiness is…

Doing what you love to do
Being where you want to be
Enjoying your life
And not wanting to change
A thing….

Smiling without a reason
Liking the current season
Listening to your heart
And cheerfully hearing
It sing….

Taking life the easy way
Treasuring it day by day
Being grateful for
What comes and goes
Without a cling…

Appreciating here and now
Knowing someway, somehow,
Things are just good
Granting your mood
A jolly swing…

*-Joan Marques*

# Index

**A**

Acceptance, 20, 45, 48, 51, 105, 115, 134
Altruism, 131, 139, 140, 143
Apoptosis, 85, 97
Appreciating, 26, 38, 58–65, 100, 101, 109, 110, 118, 128, 144
Artificial intelligence (AI), 126–128
Attitude, 1, 34, 55, 65, 67, 73, 86, 92, 93, 100, 107, 118, 123, 128, 129, 141, 143
Awakening, 20, 67, 92
Awareness, 8, 18, 22, 23, 26, 28, 30, 50, 56–58, 64, 70, 74, 84, 89, 126, 128, 134, 137, 139, 142, 143

**B**

Bias, 10–12, 16, 63
Blame, 13, 14, 16, 37, 118, 119
Breathe, 17, 19, 26
Breathing, 18, 19, 21, 24–28, 70, 101, 102, 110, 111, 124
Buddha, 20, 21, 24

Buddhism, 4, 107, 135
Burns, U., 88–91

**C**

Calm, 19, 21, 25–27, 34, 71, 79, 102, 111, 120, 124, 136
Changes, 7, 8, 11, 13, 14, 16, 23, 25, 31, 34, 37, 39, 42, 48, 56, 58, 60–65, 68, 73, 74, 78, 79, 84–86, 90–95, 97, 101–104, 110–112, 117, 119, 122, 124, 134, 138, 139, 142, 144
Choices, 6, 12, 32, 33, 37, 38, 49, 56, 59–60, 63, 65, 77, 78, 87–89, 92, 97, 105, 128, 141, 143
Chowdhury, A., 115, 116
Comfort zones, 8–10, 16, 96, 141
Commit, 49
Concentration, 55, 102, 107, 109, 111, 112
Concerns, 20, 25, 73, 84, 103, 107, 109, 111, 122
Confidence, 9, 139, 140

## Index

Contemplations, 71, 75, 77–82, 87, 88, 96, 133
Contemplative circle, 104, 112, 118
Criticism, 12, 122, 125

### E

Education, 6, 8, 57, 84, 89, 116, 134, 137, 142, 143
Efforts, 15, 37, 43, 74, 89, 107–109, 112, 115, 116, 123, 125, 129
Eightfold Path, 106–110, 112, 118
Empathy, 63, 69
Envy, 113, 114, 125, 126, 129
Expand, 9, 10, 64, 89, 96
Expectations, 33, 57, 61, 93, 127

### F

Flexibility, 60, 80, 100, 102, 134, 138, 142
Forgiveness, 46, 48, 49, 51

### G

Generating, 22, 38, 42, 43, 45–51, 60, 64, 100, 101, 110, 118, 128
Generating, Appreciating, Internalizing, and Newness (GAIN), 37–39, 50, 51, 71, 100–106, 110–112, 114–121, 123, 126–129, 140, 142, 143
Genius, 4, 5, 142, 143
Gifts, 3–6, 26, 49, 73, 86, 103
Grateful, 3–6, 13, 16, 19, 24, 33, 34, 48, 68, 69, 76, 80–82, 115, 122, 128, 144
Gratitude, 26, 28, 54, 68, 69, 76–82, 94, 101, 109, 110, 115, 116, 119, 121, 122, 125
Grit, 14, 46–51, 125
Growth, 13, 64, 85, 86, 89, 96, 97, 140

### I

Impermanence, 22, 25, 28, 51
Improvement, 64, 87, 89–96, 101, 104, 109, 110, 125, 129
Insights, 5, 7, 10, 11, 14–16, 19–23, 25–28, 33, 37, 39, 41, 49, 55, 61, 62, 64, 69, 70, 79, 84, 85, 94, 96, 101–104, 106, 107, 109, 111, 112, 119, 123, 138, 139, 142, 143
Intentions, 22, 31, 32, 42, 60, 75, 100, 101, 107–109, 112, 133
Internalizing, 26, 37, 38, 68, 71, 75–82, 85, 91, 97, 101, 110, 116, 118, 128

### J

Journaling, 103, 111, 134

### L

Lamenting, Obsessing, Scathing, Envying (LOSE), 121–126, 129
Leaders, 20, 76, 93, 114, 128, 134, 140, 142, 143
Leadershift, 138–140, 143
Left brain, 137
Lethargy, 55
Light, 2, 4, 9, 16, 34, 38, 39, 42, 49, 54–65, 68, 84, 100, 103, 110, 111, 117, 121, 126
Livelihood, 95, 107–109, 112, 119

### M

Meaning, 55, 91–97
Meditations, 15, 18–25, 28, 30, 34, 38, 68, 70, 74, 81, 84, 87, 88, 94, 101, 104, 109, 110, 112, 118, 124, 137, 143
Mentors, 10, 14, 36, 37, 43, 93, 94, 102, 104, 111, 123, 142, 143

Mind, 10, 13, 14, 16, 18, 19, 21, 23–26, 28, 31, 34, 37, 42, 45, 48, 51, 59–61, 63, 68, 70, 75, 81, 90, 94–96, 102–104, 106, 107, 109, 111, 112, 114, 117, 119–123, 126, 129, 132, 133, 135, 141–143
Mindfulness, 24, 34, 36, 74, 75, 78, 79, 81, 82, 99, 100, 107, 109, 112, 132, 134–137, 142
Mindsets, 10, 12, 23, 34, 69, 70, 86, 104, 107, 112, 115, 118, 119, 121–126, 129, 139, 140, 142, 143
Mudita, 126

N

Newness, 38, 39, 64, 75–81, 84–97, 101, 110, 116, 119, 128

O

Obsessing, 37, 39, 122–123, 129
Oneness, 23, 26, 28, 74, 77
Opportunities, 6, 8–10, 15, 16, 24, 26, 36, 37, 39, 42, 43, 45, 51, 56–59, 64, 77, 84, 86, 88, 89, 93, 100, 116, 119, 124, 125, 134
Optimism, 73, 90, 91, 93, 94, 97

P

Paradigm shifts, 76, 79, 80, 82, 87
Path, 7, 14, 15, 20, 21, 36, 38, 39, 43–45, 51, 59, 63, 64, 69, 72, 75–81, 88–97, 105, 108
Patience, 33, 36, 45, 47, 48, 51
Perspectives, 4, 10, 36, 37, 55, 59, 62–65, 69, 74, 76, 79, 81, 84, 85, 94, 96, 100, 103, 104, 107, 114–120, 128, 129, 134, 141, 142
Powell, C., 72, 73, 75, 76
Purposes, 7, 13, 20, 21, 38, 39, 42, 55, 56, 64, 70, 72, 74, 76, 96, 100, 110, 114, 134, 141, 143

R

Reality-Check, 141, 143
Reflections, 7, 10, 29, 31, 59–61, 65, 72, 101, 110
Reframing, 104, 112
Religions, 20, 69, 80, 102, 104, 106, 112, 132
Resilience, 13, 16, 36, 62, 64, 76, 80, 82, 86, 128, 139, 140
Respect, 2, 10, 23, 24, 26, 43, 47, 48, 62, 69, 70, 75, 81, 90, 94, 123, 134, 141, 142
Retrospect, 116
Right brain, 137–138, 142, 143
Roadblocks, 6–12, 16

S

Scathing, 123–125, 129
Self-renewal, 86, 90, 91, 95–97
Serenity, 14, 21, 25, 28, 48
Setbacks, 12–16, 48, 69, 87, 117
Shiva, V., 73–77
Sleepwalking, 6, 8, 16, 141
Sounding board, 104, 111, 122
Spiritual, 24, 31, 69–74, 81, 96, 102, 114, 133
Spirituality, 69
Stress, 9, 25, 28, 48, 80, 103, 111, 117, 126, 135, 138
Suffering, 21, 34, 48, 56, 59, 61, 62, 65, 79, 106, 108, 109, 112, 117, 136

## T

Thich Nhat Hanh, 24, 78, 107, 108, 114, 132

## U

Usefulness, 141, 143

## V

Vipassana, 15, 19–25, 28, 38, 70, 109

## Y

Yoga, 87, 92, 102, 104, 111, 112, 134

GPSR Compliance

The European Union's (EU) General Product Safety Regulation (GPSR) is a set of rules that requires consumer products to be safe and our obligations to ensure this.

If you have any concerns about our products, you can contact us on

ProductSafety@springernature.com

In case Publisher is established outside the EU, the EU authorized representative is:

Springer Nature Customer Service Center GmbH
Europaplatz 3
69115 Heidelberg, Germany

www.ingramcontent.com/pod-product-compliance
Lightning Source LLC
LaVergne TN
LVHW011000250326
834688LV00003B/39